SALAD GARDENS

EX LIBRIS

Ridgely

Karan Davis Cutler, Guest Editor

FOR THE ADVANCEMENT OF BOTANY AND THE SERVICE OF THE CITY

BROOKLYN BOTANIC GARDEN

PUBLICATIONS

· MCMXCV ·

Janet Marinelli
SERIES EDITOR

Anne Witte Garland
ASSOCIATE EDITOR

Bekka Lindstrom
ART DIRECTOR

Stephen K·M. Tim
VICE PRESIDENT, SCIENCE, LIBRARY & PUBLICATIONS

Judith D. Zuk
PRESIDENT

Elizabeth Scholtz
DIRECTOR EMERITUS

Handbook #144

Copyright © Autumn 1995 by the Brooklyn Botanic Garden, Inc.

BBG gardening books are published quarterly at 1000 Washington Ave., Brooklyn, NY 11225

Subscription included in Brooklyn Botanic Garden membership dues ($25.00 per year)

ISSN 0362-5850 ISBN # 0-945352-89-1

PRINTED IN KOREA

Table of Contents

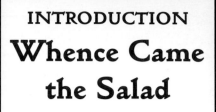

INTRODUCTION
Whence Came
the Salad

BY KARAN DAVIS CUTLER

THE SPANISH PROVERB advises that it takes four persons to make a salad: a spendthrift to measure the oil, a miser the vinegar, a counselor the salt and a madman to stir it all up. In fact, it takes one more: a gardener to grow the vegetables. However good the dressing, produce fresh from the garden is the heart of a great salad.

While eating uncooked vegetables—the definition of salad used for this book—is more fashionable than ever, it isn't new. The poet Virgil (70-19 B.C.) wrote an ode to the salad (the word comes from the Latin for salt, *sal*, a derivation originating with the Roman practice of eating greens that had been dipped in salt). Despite its ancient roots, the salad fell out of favor for centuries. Suspicion of and indifference to raw vegetables was rampant. The kitchen notebooks of Leonardo da Vinci (1452-1519), which are crammed with recipes for shoulder of serpent, pierced pigs' ears, cockscombs, trouts' intestines and leg of loon (as well as information about "Ridding your Kitchen of Pestilential Flies" and "An Alternative to Filthy Tablecloths"), give short shrift to uncooked vegetables. Da Vinci acknowledges that his cook Battista is fond of "serving me with unwashed lettuce…and this I normally give to my dog if I can without Battista seeing me."

Slowly, however, vegetables were rescued from serving solely as potherbs. The earliest English salad recipe, which dates from about 1390, is for a mixture of herbs, greens, onions and leeks. "Pick them, pluck them small with thine hand and mingle them well with raw oil. Lay on vinegar and salt and serve it forth." Elizabethans were more adventuresome, topping herbs and greens, such as lettuce, purslane, sorrel, dandelion, mustard, cress, turnip and radish greens, spinach, chicory and chives, with flowers, petals of violets, borage, primroses, gilliflowers and especially nasturtiums, a new import from the West Indies. In 1699, came John Evelyn's *Acetaria: A Discourse of Sallets*. Evelyn gave growers their due when he noted that "sallets in general consist of certain Esculent Plants and Herbs, improv'd by Culture, Industry and Art of the Gard'ner…."

Yet doubts about uncooked vegetables ran deep—tomatoes were still believed to be toxic as late at 1820, when Robert Johnson gobbled up a basketful on the steps of the Salem, New Jersey, courthouse with no immediate ill effects and settled the controversy once and for all. Forty-five years later, in the second edition of *The Field and Garden Vegetables of America*, New England horticulturist Fear-

A wealth of cultivars, both heirlooms and hybrids, is only as far away as a good seed catalog.

ing Burr not only listed 35 tomatoes, including long-lost names like 'Lester's Perfected' and 'The Cook's Favorite', but also a farmful of available salad plants, including nine varieties of chicory, 38 Romaine lettuces, 55 cucumbers, 22 endives, 46 kales, 19 parsleys, 49 radishes, 13 spinaches and 13 Swiss chards.

Although we often think of it as an invention of the late-20th century, the main-course salad emerged more than 80 years ago, promoted in women's magazines as a healthy alternative to traditional menus. "Instead of paying $2 a bottle for Dr. Whoosis Bitters for rheumatism…, we prefer to buy our blood purifiers at the vegetable stand and salad counter," one enthusiast explained in 1928. Most Americans were confirmed salad eaters by the end of World War II, due to a serendipitous conjunction of a heightened interest in health and nutrition, better methods of transportation and storage and the innovative work of plant breeders

However good the dressing, produce fresh from the garden is the heart of a great salad.

In England and Europe, the salad appears after the main course, a palate-clearing prelude to dessert. In North America, we take our salad first, a simple course to stir the appetite.

and seed importers. Today, there are hundreds of lettuces and tomatoes, scores of cucumbers, peppers, radishes and spinaches, dozens of cabbages and scallions. This wealth of cultivars, heirlooms and hybrids, is only as far away as a good seed catalog. (See Seed Sources, page 97.)

Only one nagging question remains about salads—before or after the main course? Interestingly, that debate is nearly as old as the salad itself. The Greeks, believing that lettuce cooled the body, argued that it should be eaten after the meal to offset the drinking to follow. The Romans followed this pattern (fittingly, when Adonis dies, Venus throws herself on a bed of lettuce to cool her ardor), but only until the first century A.D., when they moved the salad course to before the meal, so that it would offset the alcohol consumed *during* dinner.

It's been back and forth ever since. In 1597, the English herbalist John Gerard reported that the salad was "served in these daies, and in these countries in the beginning of supper, and eaten first before any other meat...." But in England and Europe today, the salad appears after the main course, a palate-clearing prelude to dessert; in North America, we take our salad first, a simple course to stir the appetite.

But if you grow your own salads, you'll likely follow Gerard's second bit of advice on the subject. "Now and then," he writes, it may "be eaten at both those times to the health of the body."

GETTING STARTED
Salad-garden Basics

BY KARAN DAVIS CUTLER

**W**HILE OUR ANCESTORS didn't know 'Early Girl' tomatoes or 'Red Sails' lettuce, they knew a good deal about growing salad crops. "Close to his cottage lay a garden-ground,/With reeds and osiers sparely girt around;/Small was the spot, but liberal to produce…" begins Virgil's "The Salad," a poem written 2,000 years ago. His image of a salad garden is still timely: a conveniently located small, fertile plot protected from the wind that will yield generously.

Those with land to spare can spread their lettuces, carrots and tomatoes over a half-acre or more. A 100-foot row will produce 85 pounds of onions, 120 pounds of cucumbers or 150 pounds of cabbage, but few of us need harvests this large. Fortunately, we can also farm in Mason jars, clay and plastic pots, wood tubs and raised beds that measure 2 feet by 2 or 5 feet by 20. We can tuck cabbages between daylilies and shasta daisies and cultivate chives on the windowsill. The secret to salad gardening isn't how *large* the growing area, but how *good*.

Except in hot regions, where protection from the afternoon sun is sometimes necessary, most salad crops do best in full sun. For gardeners with a less-than-perfect location, it's a relief to know that some crops, including beets, carrots, chives, cress, endive, looseleaf lettuce, parsley, radishes, scallions, spinach and turnips, will succeed with only five or six hours of direct sunlight a day. All plants prefer to be out of the wind, though they also want good air circulation, which will help them ward off diseases. "Evil aire," warned Thomas Hill, the author of *The Gardener's Labyrinth* (1577), "doth not only annoy and corrupt the plants…but choke and dul the spirits of men." And women.

Hill also talked about water, not only the need for adequate moisture but the need for well-drained soil. Ground where "the watriness shall exceed" will dash a gardener's enthusiasm faster than an invasion of Japanese beetles. Carrying water isn't much fun either, so try to locate your garden near a water source if you know it is unlikely to receive the one inch per week of rain that most vegetables need.

The secret to salad gardening isn't how large the growing area, but how good. Most salad crops do best in well-drained soil in full sun, protected from the wind but with good air circulation to prevent disease.

Follow the recommendations on seed packets for planting depths and spacing. Seeds sown too deep will rot, and plants set too close together will never have a chance to develop fully.

SOIL BASICS

Soil pH. While we'd all wish for humus-rich loam, the chances of getting it are about as good as catching wind in a net. Before you begin amending and enriching, however, it's smart to determine what you have. Most vegetables do fine with a pH between 6.0 and 7.0. The majority of soils fall in that range, so a pH test probably isn't necessary unless you suspect yours is highly acid or alkaline. But it is useful to analyze your soil makeup with a simple "jar" test: Take a half-cup of garden soil—dug vertically like a core sample—and place it and about two cups of water into a straight-sided clear-glass jar. Screw on the lid and shake. When the sample settles, it should be nicely layered: The sand will rest on the bottom, the silt above it, clay atop the silt, and the organic material will float on the surface. You can measure and calculate the exact percentage of each, or just eyeball it to know whether you're working with sand or clay. Mostly sand? More humus will give it body. Mostly clay? More humus will open it up.

Fertilizer. In addition to friable soil, plants need an assortment of chemical elements. Three of the half dozen most important—carbon, hydrogen and oxygen—are available from air and water, but the remaining big three must be supplied by the soil: nitrogen (N), which promotes quick growth and deep green foliage; phosphorus (P), essential to root development and flower and seed production; and potassium (K), which helps plants resist disease and cold and aids fruit production. Most salad crops grow best in moderately rich soil that has an equal supply of nitrogen, phosphorus and potassium. Many gardeners overdo the fertilizer, though; if you regularly add compost and other organic matter to your garden, no additional fertilizers should be necessary. And by adding humus you'll be improving the soil's tilth at the same time. The ancient—and wise—rule is to feed the soil, not the plant. When earthworms become plentiful, it's a safe bet that your soil is healthy.

Preparing the ground. For cold-loving crops like peas, it's a good idea to prepare the ground the previous fall. I use a spading fork to turn the section of my vegetable patch that will be planted first, then cover it with shredded maple leaves mixed with horse manure, which will break down over the winter. In spring, as soon as I can get in the garden (the traditional test is to squeeze a fistful of soil—if it forms a firm sticky ball, it's still too

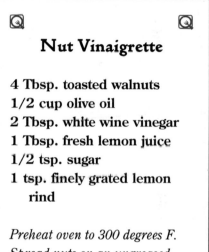

Nut Vinaigrette

4 Tbsp. toasted walnuts
1/2 cup olive oil
2 Tbsp. white wine vinegar
1 Tbsp. fresh lemon juice
1/2 tsp. sugar
1 tsp. finely grated lemon
rind

Preheat oven to 300 degrees F. Spread nuts on an ungreased baking sheet and toast for about 5 minutes (do not let scorch). Remove from oven and cool. In a small bowl, combine olive oil and 1 Tbsp. coarsely chopped nuts. Let stand 1 hour. Strain oil into a jar and add vinegar, lemon juice, sugar and rind. Cover and shake until ingredients are mixed. Sprinkle salad with the remaining 3 Tbsp. nuts.

early to be gardening), I scratch in what mulch remains with a cultivator and plant. The rest of the garden is turned in the spring. If you use a rototiller, as I do, don't get carried away. Garden soil is not improved by being pulverized to the consistency of river sand.

PLANTING AND TRANSPLANTING

Sowing and thinning. Most seed packets provide recommendations for planting depths and spacing. Take them seriously. Seeds sown too deep will rot, especially in cold, wet soil, and plants set too close together will never have a chance to develop fully. That's not a great problem with lettuces—you can harvest six small plants rather than one large one—but carrots or radishes that are crowded will fail to form roots. It's painful to rip out healthy young seedlings, but close your eyes if you must, take a deep breath and yank.

CROP FAMILIES

Crop rotation helps the soil and reduces pest and disease problems. Avoid planting members of the same plant family in the same spot year after year.

CHENOPODIACEAE	CRUCIFERAE	LEGUMINOSAE
chard	broccoli	bean
beet	cabbage	pea
orach	cauliflower	
spinach	Chinese cabbage	LILIACEAE
	cress	chive
COMPOSITAE	kale	garlic
chicory	mizuna	onion
dandelion	mustard	scallion
endive	radish	
escarole	turnip	SOLANACEAE
Jerusalem artichoke		pepper
lettuce	CUCURBITACEAE	tomato
radicchio	cucumber	
	squash	UMBELLIFERAE
		carrot
		celery
		parsley

Many gardeners overdo the fertilizer. If you regularly add compost and other organic matter to your garden, no additional fertilizers should be necessary.

Salad crops that begin their careers indoors, such as tomatoes and peppers, need an early start but not a *too*-early start. Plants sown prematurely become weak and leggy, so err on the late side, and don't begin tomatoes and peppers more than six weeks before the frost-free date, especially if you're gardening on a windowsill and not under artificial lights. I use standard-sized 10-by-20-inch trays filled with tapered cells—small, medium and large, depending on the crop—and a potting mix I put together with equal parts compost, garden soil and perlite. Any planting containers will do—clay pots, milk cartons, Styrofoam coffee cups, pie pans—as long as they have bottom drainage and aren't excessively large. Two basil seeds are lost in a 10-inch pot filled with damp soil.

Commercial seedling mixes work as well as my home-made potting soil. Just be sure the medium you use is sterile—waking up to a flat of toppled seedlings,

Whether you plant in tidy rows, broadcast seeds in beds or garden in raised beds or containers, intercropping and succession planting will help ensure a steady supply of salads. Tuck small vegetables between larger ones.

victims of the "damping off" fungus, is as discouraging as discovering woodchucks have moved into your garden. Keep the soil damp and provide plenty of warmth, at least 65° F, to speed germination. Once the seedlings emerge, move the flats to a spot where they will receive bright light but are away from cold drafts or drying heat. Water carefully—keeping the soil moist but not wet—and feed as needed. If you've sown in a nutrient-poor medium, such as vermiculite, peat or perlite, the plants will need to be fertilized: water twice a week with a weak solution of fish emulsion (two teaspoons emulsion to one gallon water). And thin, removing all

One form of succession planting involves sowing in spaces vacated by other crops. Be aware of each plant's root requirements and plant shallow-rooted plants with deeper-rooted vegetables.

misshapen or weak plants first, then enough plants to eliminate crowding.

Transplanting. If you've been a real early bird, your seedlings will need to be transplanted to larger, deeper containers before it's time to take them outdoors. Handle them gently as you move them to larger quarters, and provide them with the richer soil they now need. Most salad crops transplant well, but carrots, cucumbers, spinach, summer squash, Swiss chard and turnips are fussy, so take extra care not to disturb their roots, and avoid handling any seedling by its stem. But don't avoid handling it: Research shows that seedlings that have

15

been gently brushed every day (use your hand or a piece of paper) are stockier and stronger than those left untouched.

Ten days before a plant goes into the garden is the time for "hardening off," the horticultural equivalent of adjusting to leaving home. Many gardeners use cold frames for this process, but I simply move my flats to a shaded, protected location on my patio for three or four hours, then bring them back inside. Each day I extend their time outdoors and expose them to increasing amounts of sun and wind. By the time I'm ready to plant them into the garden, they're spending both day and night outside.

Save an evening to plant out, or take advantage of an overcast day. Most salad vegetables should be set slightly deeper than the depth they were growing in their pot, and tomatoes should be buried at least half-way up their stem. After you firm the soil around the transplant, water it with a weak solution of fish emulsion and provide some protection from sun and wind for the first three or four days.

> The juice [of onions] annointed upon a pild or bald head in the Sun, bringeth the haire again very speedily.
>
> John Gerard,
> *The Herball, or Historie of Plants,*
> *1597*

INCREASING YOUR YIELDS

Whether you plant in tidy rows, broadcast seed in beds or garden in containers, two techniques will help ensure a steady supply of salads: succession planting and interplanting. One form of succession planting involves sowing in spaces vacated by other crops—planting a row of beans, for example, where the radishes had been—or planting short- and long-season crops, such as radishes and beans, together. The radishes will be pulled long before the beans demand all the space. Succession planting also refers to making small plantings every week or ten days, rather than one large planting. Lettuce, scallions and beans are among the salad vegetables that can be planted in succession. Many crops, such as spinach and peas, can be sown again in midsummer for a fall harvest. Breeders have made succession planting even easier by producing "early" and "late" varieties. I can set

Don't limit intercropping to the vegetable patch. Many salad crops are wonderfully ornamental, and can join the true ornamentals in your flower garden.

out 'Earliana' (60 days), 'Early Round Dutch' (80 days) and 'Apex' (100 days) on the same day in early spring and harvest cabbage from June until October.

Interplanting, or intercropping, is another way to have a constant supply of salad vegetables and also to increase your garden's yields. Small vegetables can be tucked between larger ones—onions mixed in a bed of broccoli or spinach. When you're mixing plants in a single bed or row, be aware of each plant's root requirements: Shallow-rooted plants, such as garlic, endive or spinach, are best matched with deeper-rooted vegetables like tomatoes. Or combine large sun-loving plants, such as tomatoes or peppers, with shade-tolerant leaf crops like lettuce or spinach, which will benefit from the shadows thrown by their taller partners. Finally, don't limit intercropping to the vegetable patch. Many salad crops are wonderfully ornamental—lettuces, cabbages and kales come immediately to mind—and can join the true ornamentals in your flower garden.

Still another way of increasing yields is to do what cities have done—grow up. Cucumbers are natural candidates for trellising. Training the vines to ascend not only saves room, but also produces straighter, cleaner cucumbers and, according to more than one study, actually increases the number of fruits. Tomatoes should be staked or caged, rather than left to sprawl, and other vining plants, such as Malabar spinach and peas, do their best when allowed to follow their natural bent and climb.

A last method of expanding the harvest, at least for northern gardeners, is to extend it through the use of insulating covers, such as cold frames, plastic-covered tunnels, floating row covers and heavy mulches. Eliot Coleman's *The New Organic Grower's Four-Season Harvest* (see Further Reading, page 104) is the last word on the topic, the essential reference for salad gardeners who want to harvest lettuce, spinach and carrots long after common sense deems it possible. The *growing* season, Coleman explains, is limited to the warmer months, but there are no limits on the *harvest* season. I cry "uncle" in November, long after the first frost, but *Four-Season Harvest* makes clear that I could be cutting parsley in December, January and even March, if I wanted to.

CLOSING DOWN

The work isn't over when the last turnip is pulled. Then it's time to think ahead—to prepare and enrich the soil for next year's salads. After cleaning up the garden—especially spent tomato plants, which harbor diseases—I sow a "green manure," a cover crop of rye or red clover. It squeezes out weeds in late fall, protects the soil in winter and, when tilled under in May, enriches the soil. Any part of the garden not planted with a green manure I blanket with at least 6 inches of mulch—a mix of compost, shredded leaves, hay and horse manure.

This is the time, too, for planning next year's garden, taking care to rotate the placement of my salad crops. Crop rotation not only helps the soil, it reduces problems from diseases and pests. The basic rule is not to locate the same thing in the same place year after year. Better still, avoid planting a spot with another member of the same plant *family*—preferably for three or four years, but at least for a year. Tomatoes and peppers are both members of the family Solanaceae, so I don't plant peppers where the tomatoes grew last year. Instead, I'll put the cucumbers where the tomatoes grew, and plant peppers where the peas were. (See "Crop Families," page 12).

Take care to rotate the placement of salad crops. Crop rotation not only helps the soil, but also reduces problems from disease and pests.

As the snow piles up outside, I plow through the mail-order seed catalogs (see Seed Sources, page 97). They offer variety that isn't available at the local garden center, everything from new-minted F_1 hybrids to open-pollinated old timers, such as 'Black-Seeded Simpson' lettuce and 'Dinner Plate' tomato. Disease resistance ranks high on my list of priorities, so I'm on the lookout for abbreviations such as "VF," which indicates that the variety is resistant to verticillium and fusarium wilts. And I take advantage of regional seed companies, firms that specialize in cultivars that will thrive in my near-Arctic conditions. Then I take a serious look at my orders, admit that my family couldn't possibly consume 19 different lettuces, 13 radishes, 11 tomatoes, 9 beans, 9 cucumbers, 8 carrots, 6 peas, 5 spinaches, 4 scallions, 3 peppers, 3 summer squash and an assortment of other greens, and I cut the order by two-thirds. A salad, after all, is a simple thing.

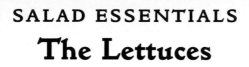

SALAD ESSENTIALS
The Lettuces

BY DEBORAH WECHSLER

LETTUCE (*Lactuca sativa*) is the backbone of the salad, the dependable base to which other flavors and textures are added. Because of its commercial dominance, iceberg lettuce, with its pale crispy sameness, has become the stereotypical lettuce. Yet in the garden, lettuce has always struck me as having a frivolous and ornamental personality—a quick-growing, shallow-rooted plant with a showy appearance and delicate texture. A frilly vegetable lace. Every spring, as green begins to overtake the grays and browns of winter, my lettuce patch is bedecked in a profusion of colors and shapes, from light green ruffles to dark, smooth curves to bicolored crinkles of red and green.

Until the 1920s, lettuce was exclusively a local crop, not well adapted to shipping, and many kinds of looseleaf, Romaine and loosely headed lettuces were grown and sold locally. By 1948, when 'Great Lakes', the first true iceberg lettuce, was released, our lettuce habits had changed. Head lettuces dominated. Packed in ice and shipped by rail from commercial farms in the South and West, they replaced non-heading varieties. Home gardeners now switched to the harder-to-grow icebergs or contented themselves with less fashionable leaf types. Then, about 15 years ago, discerning cooks and seed companies rediscovered non-heading lettuces. While iceberg lettuce hasn't gone the way of the hoop skirt, many more interesting lettuces are increasingly popular—and available.

Lettuce isn't strongly flavored, except when it turns bitter, and the flavors of different lettuces don't vary greatly (of all lettuces, Romaines have the most taste). And while the blanched inner leaves of any heading lettuce are lower in vitamin A than the darker outer leaves, no lettuce scores high nutritionally. The real pleasures of lettuce, both in the garden and the salad, are its textures and visual variety. Choose varieties according to their adaptability to your climate and conditions, and your own preferences for color and texture. Explore diversity. (See page 24 for descriptions of dozens of lettuce varieties.)

Every spring, as green begins to overtake the grays and browns of winter, the lettuce patch is bedecked in a profusion of colors and shapes, from light green ruffles to dark, smooth curves to bicolored crinkles of red and green.

A LETTUCE PRIMER

'Red Sails' with the slow-to-bolt 'Simpson Elite'

Looseleaf Lettuces. Looseleaf, or cutting, lettuces are the easiest and quickest to grow, maturing in about 45 days. They can be harvested leaf by leaf ("cut and come again") or you can cut a whole plant. There are three major styles of looseleaf foliage. Of the green lettuces with wavy, crinkly leaves and smooth but curly margins, my favorite is the old timer 'Black Seeded Simpson'. It's particularly quick-growing, about 45 days, and I like its light green color and relaxed waviness. 'Simpson Elite', which is described as an "improved" version but is actually a different variety entirely, is slower to bolt (go to seed) and more uniform, but I find its tighter, more savoyed, or crinkled, leaf shape less pleasing. The second common looseleaf lettuce style is defined by deeply indented leaves like an oak's. The leaves are tender and delicate, and the plants are slow-bolting and mild-flavored, even in hot weather. Finally, there are several extremely frilly and decorative European varieties, as deeply curled as an ornamental kale.

'Rosy', like other crisphead lettuces, has a crisp, sweet, juicy crunch.

Chrisphead Lettuces. Crisphead, or iceberg, lettuce is the hardest type to grow successfully. The densely packed heads take about 80 days to develop, almost twice as long as looseleaf lettuces. If they are subjected to water or nutritional stress at any time during their growth, they head up prematurely and poorly. While head lettuce is disparaged for its lack of flavor and nutritional value, it still has a legitimate role for its crisp, sweet, juicy crunch. Standard home garden varieties include 'Ithaca' and 'Great Lakes'; a good red crisphead (though the inner leaves are still white) is 'Rosy', a small variety that is slow to bolt. 'Summertime', new in 1994, withstands heat better than other crispheads and is a superior choice for home gardeners.

Butterhead leaves really do feel buttery.

Butterhead Lettuces. Butterhead is the name that has been given to all the soft, round-leaved, loosely headed types. (They are also called bibb or Boston lettuces, after two old cultivars.) Butterhead is a good name: The leaves really do feel buttery. Inner foliage is blanched yellow and slightly crisp. Butterhead lettuces are easier to grow than crispheads and mature in 55 to 65 days. One of the best home-garden varieties is the dark green 1963 All-America Selections (AAS) winner 'Butter-crunch'. Recently there's been an explosion in choices, including some gorgeous bicolors. Many of these are imported from Europe, where butterheads are the most popular type of lettuce. Well-known bicolors include my favorite, 'Sangria', a medium-sized cultivar that is resistant to downy mildew. 'Tom Thumb', a "baby" butterhead dating from the 19th century, is perfect for a windowbox garden.

Romaine lettuce ribs are tender and crunchy.

Romaine Lettuces. Romaine, or cos, lettuce is a tall head type with long, spoon-shaped leaves and thick midribs. The names are interchangeable, both deriving from the plant's Mediterranean origin: "Romaine" is a corruption of Roman, while cos comes from Kos, the Greek island. Standard Romaines mature in 60 to 75 days; miniature varieties are ready to harvest a little sooner. Outer leaves of Romaines can be a bit tough, but the ribs are tender and crunchy, the flavor is sweet, and the leaves are nicely sandwich-shaped. 'Parris Island Cos' is a tall, widely adapted variety; in North Carolina, where I garden, market gardeners prefer 'Romulus' for its sweeter flavor. 'Little Gem' is a smaller home-garden favorite with outstanding flavor. Good red varieties include the medium-sized 'Rosalita' bred by Johnny's Select Seeds in Maine, and the French heirloom 'Rouge d'Hiver'. 'Winter Density', a kind of a bibb-Romaine cross, has good flavor and is especially frost tolerant, making it a good choice for fall sowing.

Batavian Lettuces. Batavians (also called French crisps or summer crisps) are a relatively unfamiliar group of lettuces with many advantages. They can be harvested early as looseleafs, but if left to mature, develop tight, compact heads or bunches, which are crisp and juicy. Better still, they mature more quickly than crispheads (55 to 60 days), are more heat tolerant and are easier to grow. 'Reine des Glaces' is an elegant French import, slow-bolting with a slightly nutty flavor.

GROWING LETTUCE

Lettuce likes cool weather, with temperatures between 50° and 60° F, and germinates best at soil temperatures of 60° to 75°. When soil temperatures climb over 80° (which can easily happen in the top half-inch of soil even when air

LETTUCES FOR THE SALAD GARDEN

	TYPE	DAYS/MATURITY
'BLACK SEEDED SIMPSON'	L	45
'BRONZE ARROW'	L	50
'BRUNE D'HIVER'	B	55
'BUTTERCRUNCH'	B	65
'CANASTA'	BA	50
'CAPITANE'	B	65
'DEER TONGUE'	L	55
'ERMOSA'	B	50
'GRAND RAPIDS'	L	50
'GREAT LAKES'	C	80
'GREEN ICE'	L	45
'GREEN MIGNONETTE'	B	65
'ITHACA'	C	75
'KRISTIA'	BA	60
'LITTLE GEM'	R	70
'LOLLO BIONDO'	L	50
'LOLLO ROSSA'	L	52
'MAY QUEEN'	B	60
'MAJESTIC RED'	R	50
KEY: B=BUTTERHEAD, BA=BATAVIAN, C=CRISPHEAD, L=LOOSELEAF, R=ROMAINE		

and general soil temperatures are much lower), germination drops to almost nothing. Planting when the soil is too hot is one of the most common mistakes made by home gardeners. If the soil has already warmed, either start seeds in flats in a cool spot, or cover the seedrow with a board (a 2x6 board is both thick and wide enough). Always plant lettuce seeds shallowly— about 1/8 to 1/4 inch deep. Lettuce transplants well, so resetting seedlings into the garden is easy. Plants spaced 10 to 12 inches apart will reach their

Herb Mayonnaise

1/2 cup prepared mayonnaise
2 tsp. white wine vinegar
1 Tbsp. fresh minced parsley
1 Tbsp. fresh minced herb, such as dill, chive or basil
1 tsp. water (optional)

Combine all ingredients in a small bowl. Whisk until blended. If desired, thin with water.

COLOR	NOTES
LIGHT GREEN	HEIRLOOM
REDDISH-BROWN	HEIRLOOM OAKLEAF
BROWNISH-RED	EXTREMELY HARDY
DARK GREEN	HEAT RESISTANT
RED/GREEN	BOLT RESISTANT
GREEN	LARGE AND VIGOROUS
GREEN	HEIRLOOM OAKLEAF
GREEN	HEAT TOLERANT
LIGHT GREEN	MILDEW RESISTANT
GREEN	ICEBERG TYPE
GREEN	BOLT RESISTANT
GREEN	ADAPTED FOR HOT CLIMATES
GREEN	HEAT RESISTANT; WIDELY GROWN
GREEN	GOOD HEAT TOLERANCE
GREEN	OUTSTANDING FLAVOR
GREEN	GOOD CUTTING LETTUCE
GREEN/RED FRINGES	DEEPLY CURLED; HEAT TOLERANT
GREEN	HEIRLOOM
RED	COMPACT, HEAT AND DROUGHT RESISTANT

CONTINUES ON THE NEXT PAGE...

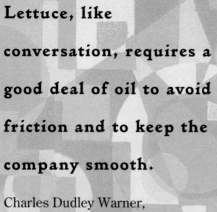

Lettuce, like conversation, requires a good deal of oil to avoid friction and to keep the company smooth.

Charles Dudley Warner,
My Summer in a Garden, 1871

full size and glory; if you plant more closely, you will need to thin as the plants grow. Direct-seeded plants are usually set far too close together—seed sparingly and thin (and eat) young plants.

Year-round Harvest. It's possible to have lettuce virtually year-round in many parts of the country. If protected from wind, most lettuces can survive temperatures as low as 15°. Here in North Carolina, I grow lettuce all winter, either under floating row covers or in an unheated cold-

	TYPE	DAYS/MATURITY
'MERVEILLE DES QUATRE SAISONS'	B	65
'MISSION'	C	75
'MONTELLO'	C	75
'NANCY'	B	58
'OAKLEAF'	L	45
'PARRIS ISLAND COS'	R	68
'PIRAT'	B	55
'PRIZEHEAD'	L	50
'RED FIRE'	L	45
'RED GRENOBLE'	BA	48
'RED OAK LEAF'	L	50
'RED RIDING HOOD'	B	65
'RED SAILS'	L	45
'RED SALAD BOWL'	L	45
'REINE DES GLACES'	BA	62
'ROMANCE'	R	50
'ROMULUS'	R	59
'ROSALITA'	R	62
'ROSY'	C	70
'ROUGE D'HIVER'	R	68
'RUBENS DWARF'	R	58
KEY: B=BUTTERHEAD, BA=BATAVIAN, C=CRISPHEAD, L=LOOSELEAF, R=ROMAINE		

frame. Even in northern regions, lettuce overwinters fairly well under a cover and a few inches of insulating snow. Heat is more of a problem, though the most crucial factor for lettuce is regular, adequate watering. If your garden heats up in summer, be sure to plant slow-bolting, heat-tolerant varieties. And grow them in partial shade (under a tree, beneath a bean teepee, in the shade of a tomato trellis, under shadecloth or lattice).

Succession planting—sowing small quantities of seeds frequently—is the secret to a regular supply of good lettuce. Market gardeners plant as often as every four or five days and stop picking one planting when the next is ready, even though the first may still look good. Sowing seeds every two weeks is a good schedule for home gardeners. I sometimes start seeds in flats and direct seed at the same time, figuring that the plantings won't mature at the same time.

Pests and Diseases. While lettuce attracts fewer bugs and diseases than most vegetable crops, it's not indestructible. The most pervasive pests are slugs

COLOR	NOTES
RED/GREEN	QUICK-HEADING FRENCH HEIRLOOM
GREEN	HEAT TOLERANT
GREEN	STANDARD ICEBERG
GREEN	LARGE HEADS
GREEN	OLD VARIETY; HEAT RESISTANT
GREEN	TALL; HEADS WELL
RED/GREEN	BOLT RESISTANT; COMPACT
RED/GREEN	CRISP, SWEET
RED	WITHSTANDS HEAT & COLD
RED TINGED	VERY COLD RESISTANT
RED	TURNS REDDER IN FULL SUN
REDDISH	LARGE HEADS
RED	COMPACT; MILD FLAVOR
RED	OAKLEAF TYPE; BOLT RESISTANT
GREEN	HEIRLOOM; NUTTY FLAVOR
GREEN	LARGE, FAST GROWING
GREEN	SWEET FLAVOR
RED	NOT FOR WARM CLIMATES
RED	SMALL; SLOW TO BOLT
RED	HEIRLOOM
RED	12-INCH HEADS
CONTINUES ON THE NEXT PAGE...	

'Lollo Rossa' and 'Lollo Biondo'

and aphids. You can help discourage the first by not mulching your plants, and control the second with insecticidal soaps. There are mildew-resistant varieties, such as 'Grand Rapids' and 'Valmaine', if your garden harbors funguses, but there are many strains of mildew and most varieties are resistant to only a few. Plants that become seriously infected should be removed. Mottled yellowed leaves and stunted growth are signs of mosaic virus, which cannot be cured. Destroy any infected plants, and make sure to obtain mosaic-free seeds, which are often labeled MTO in seed catalogues, for replanting. Aphids transmit the virus, so control them with insecticidal soap. Rots, usually of leaves and crown at the soil line, are a problem in wet, poorly drained

	TYPE	DAYS/MATURITY
'RUBY'	L	48
'SALAD BOWL'	L	50
'SALINA'	B	60
'SANGRIA'	B	58
'SIERRA'	BA	60
'SIMPSON ELITE'	L	50
'SLOBOLT'	L	48
'SUMMERTIME'	C	68
'TANGO'	L	45
'TENNIS BALL'	B	70
'TOM THUMB'	B	65
'WALDMANN'S DARK GREEN'	L	50
'WINTER DENSITY'	R	65
'VALMAINE'	R	72
'VERANO'	BA	58
'VICTORIA'	BA	52
'VULCAN'	L	45
'YEDIKULE'	R	60

KEY: B=BUTTERHEAD, BA=BATAVIAN, C=CRISPHEAD, L=LOOSELEAF, R=ROMAINE

soils. Browning of leaf margins in hot weather is often caused by long exposure to sunlight; the solution is to give the plants some shade. A more serious physiological disorder is tipburn, in which the tips of leaves inside the head are brown and papery because the uptake of calcium doesn't keep up with growth. Grow tipburn-tolerant varieties, such as 'Salad Bowl' and 'Salina', and provide enough water and nutrients to the soil.

You can pick and eat lettuce as soon as you like—a salad of 2-inch-tall thinnings is tender and delicious, though hard to wash. I like to pick some of the almost-outer leaves as the plants grow, then cut full-grown plants when they mature—a large head is such a pleasure to carry from the garden and a great gift for a friend. If you wait until the stem starts to lengthen—you can see this happening easily in Romaines and looseleaf lettuces, less so in the rounder heads—the lettuce already will have started to become bitter.

Harvest on time, however, and your lettuces will be tender and flavorful. For such a garden staple, lettuce is ephemeral. Just keep planting for a sweet supply.

COLOR	NOTES
DARK RED	HEAT RESISTANT; HEAVILY CRINKLED
GREEN	TIPBURN TOLERANT; BOLT RESISTANT
GREEN	"MINI" VARIETY
RED/GREEN	MEDIUM SIZED, DOWNY MILDEW RESISTANT
RED TINGED	OPEN HEADED
GREEN	BOLT RESISTANT
LIGHT GREEN	BRED FOR WARM REGIONS
GREEN	HEAT TOLERANT
GREEN	NOT HEAT TOLERANT
GREEN	EXTREMELY HARDY
GREEN	SMALL; GOOD FOR WINDOWBOX
GREEN	VIGOROUS PRODUCTION
GREEN	BIBB-ROMAINE CROSS, FROST TOLERANT
GREEN	MILDEW RESISTANT
GREEN/RED	HEAT RESISTANT AND TENDER
GREEN	UNUSUALLY SWEET
RED/GREEN	HEAT TOLERANT
GREEN	EXTREMELY HEAT RESISTANT

BEYOND LETTUCES
The Other Greens

BY PAUL DUNPHY

LETTUCE COMES IMMEDIATELY TO MIND when most people think about a garden salad, and understandably so. Mild in flavor and tender in texture, freshly picked lettuce is lovely. If it were more tolerant of hot weather, gardeners might never look further. But when lettuce is languishing under the midsummer sun—or when you simply want to enliven a salad—it's happy news that there is an almost endless variety of other greens to grow, some familiar and many undeservedly obscure.

Admittedly, not all garden greens are as salad-friendly as lettuce. Many have a tangy or nutty flavor or a touch of bitterness. Others are downright chewy. A taste for some of these plants must be acquired, but adventurous spirits will be rewarded with a complexity of flavors. Even more immediately apparent than flavor is the visual splash of combining leaves from a dozen different plants. "Greens" becomes a figurative term when describing a salad of chards, amaranth and radicchio, with their leaves ranging from dusky blue to saffron to burgundy red. Reaching beyond lettuce can extend the salad season not only through the heat of summer but also into the early winter in northern gardens, and throughout the year in areas with little or no freezing weather.

Salad greens can be divided into two categories: those that prosper in cool weather and those that thrive in the heat. No matter which type of plant, harvest the leaves while they are young and tender. And, especially in the summer, pick them in the morning, before their vitality has been sapped by the day's heat. To maintain a supply of small leaves, sow early and often. Finally, most greens need or prefer to be grown in organically rich soil and watered attentively.

COOL-WEATHER GREENS

Spinach (*Spinacia oleracea*)

Perhaps the most widely appreciated of the cool-weather leaf vegetables is spinach. It can be grown in the spring, fall and winter in the South and through the early summer and early fall in the North. But once hot weather arrives, spinach will bolt, or go to seed, and lose its agreeable flavor. Covering plants or placing them where they will get afternoon shade, perhaps from taller crops, will delay but won't deter bolting.

"Greens" becomes a figurative term when describing a salad with leaves ranging from dusky blue to saffron to burgundy red.

Top: Japanese red mustard. Mizuna, below, germinates and grows quickly.

I get started as soon as the ground can be worked, as much as four weeks before the frost-free date, and sow the large smooth seeds 1/2 inch deep, one seed every 3 inches. Once the plants' leaves begin to touch, I thin to a spacing of 6 inches. By that time, the culls are large enough to use. Plants that are left to mature should be harvested, leaf by leaf, from the outside. Don't pull the entire plant until it begins to bolt. Within about five weeks of being sown, two dozen plants will produce enough leaves each day to make up a third of a salad for four people.

Spinach thrives in soil rich in nitrogen and iron. Blood meal added to the bed before the planting is one source of these nutrients. Spinach is often visited by flea beetles—hard, dark, shiny insects that hop among the plants and riddle the leaves with holes. Usually an outbreak lasts only about two weeks and doesn't badly damage a crop; however, severe infestations can be reduced with sticky traps. Leaf miners may also pose a threat to your crop in late spring. Larvae hatch from small, white eggs laid underneath the foliage and, like tiny moles, tunnel passages between the top and bottom surfaces

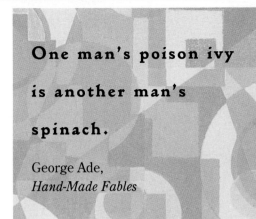

One man's poison ivy is another man's spinach.

George Ade,
Hand-Made Fables

of the leaves. Infested leaves, distinguished by a network of raised lines or gray papery patches, should be removed. Covering the crop with a lightweight row cover during the first four to six weeks of the season can prevent leaf miner flies from reaching the plants to lay their eggs.

'Melody' and 'Tyee' are two of my favorite spinach varieties, hybrids that retain their eating quality even as they begin to bolt. Both have crinkled, or savoyed, leaves, which means that they must be assiduously washed. 'Bloomsdale Long Standing' is an old open-pollinated variety with wonderfully thick, crinkled leaves; 'Winter Bloomsdale', another savoyed cultivar, is especially hardy, whereas 'Estivato' is particularly heat-resistant. 'America Giant Nobel' produces great fronds of smooth foliage but is sensitive to heat, so plant it early.

Arugula (*Eruca sativa, E. versicaria* ssp. *sativa*)

The flavor of arugula can be more peppery than many palates appreciate, but one seed merchant claims that arugula "grown well and gathered at the right moment adds a fullness to salads that will alter history" in your garden and kitchen. Such assertions might be dismissed as the hyperbolic prose of marketing, but arugula, picked young and combined judiciously with other greens, provides a distinctive taste and blue-green color that well may change your standards of what a salad should be. A member of the mustard family, arugula boasts a continental lineage and is equally well known by its Italian-derived name (from *ruca* or *rucula*) and by its French appellation, *roquette*. By one account, its seeds were first brought to North America in 1631 by the son of the Puritan leader John Winthrop, a curious beginning given the plant's contemporary association with upscale nouvelle cuisine.

To maintain a steady supply of arugula into midsummer, I plant several seeds outdoors every two weeks, beginning as soon as I can get into the garden. I thin

Bok-Choy is a member of the mustard family. Kale (below) is a mustard relative that has the distinction of being the most nutritious cultivated green.

the rosette-shaped plants to about 6 inches and begin harvesting when the deeply lobed leaves are 3 to 4 inches long—at about five weeks—either by pulling entire plants or by breaking off individual leaves. If you cut a plant off at the soil line, rather than pull it, it will resprout. As the weather warms and the plants stretch up and set their white flowers, the leaves become very sharp.

Seeds for arugula are usually sold under the common names, but there is at least one named variety called

'Sylvetta', which was selected for greater tolerance of warm weather. Smaller than the species, 'Sylvetta' has more deeply lobed leaves and yellow rather than white flowers.

Chicory (*Cichorium intybus*)

The daisy family, which includes chicory, is large and varied, but its most celebrated member for stylish salads is red chicory, or radicchio. Its ruby foliage is veined in swirls of white or pale green like elegant marble, and its flavor is almost as memorable as its appearance, though a tad more bitter than beautiful. Cultivation for some varieties is a little involved, but Dutch breeders have introduced a strain that is simpler to grow. This crop brings both vibrancy and a sense of horticultural accomplishment to the table.

Radicchio is cold hardy and insect resistant; unlike lettuce and spinach, it also stores well for weeks in the refrigerator. Some strains have been cultivated for several hundred years in northern Italy. There, and in parts of the United States where winter temperatures don't dip below 10° F, it can be planted in the fall for a late spring crop. More commonly, gardeners plant in late spring and harvest in the fall.

The small, tightly heading 'Rossa di Verona' or the more elongated Romaine-like 'Rossa di Treviso' are often planted in May or June. Seedlings should be thinned to about one foot and given some shade during midsummer. Surprisingly, their foliage is a dark, almost muddy green through most of the summer. About mid August, or after the first frost in northern gardens, cut away the outer growth, leaving only the curled fingers of foliage at the heart of the plant. As the temperatures fall, the leaf color will darken to burgundy, and the leaves will form heads.

'Giulio', a representative of the Dutch strain, forms heads without being cut back in late summer. Adapted to mild climates, it can be planted every two

---

Orange Vinaigrette

1 clove garlic
3 Tbsp. chopped fresh
  parsley
2 Tbsp. safflower oil
1-1/2 tsp. white vinegar
6 Tbsp. fresh orange juice
Salt and freshly ground
  pepper

In a food processor, mince garlic. Add parsley, oil and vinegar and pulse, just to mix. With processor running, gradually add orange juice. Salt and pepper to taste.

---

weeks or so through midsummer, and successive crops will ripen every 10 to 12 weeks thereafter—compact, round, wine-colored heads ready for the salad bowl. Other good cultivars include 'Cesare', which matures in about 90 days, and 'Chioggia', which is a red and white variegated radicchio that colors when the weather becomes cold.

HEAT-TOLERANT GREENS

Chard (*Beta vulgaris* ssp. *cicla*)
Chard not only flourishes through the heat of summer, but in many parts of the country it also will endure considerable cold, thereby providing greens over many months. Most varieties are known as Swiss chard and have a fibrous stalk or stem. For salads, the leaves should be picked when only a few inches long. Another type, less widely known but preferable for salad, is called "cutting chard" or "spinach beet." Bred for leaves rather than rib, which is thin, cutting chard remains tender and mild-flavored even when its foliage is large.

In the North, sow seeds at least two weeks before the last expected frost; in the deep South, a second planting in early June is worthwhile because the first crop may languish in July's heat. I set seeds 4 inches apart and thin the plants as they grow until they are spaced about every 10 inches. Chard is bothered by few insects or diseases and thrives in most garden soils. And it has a genetic advantage over annual greens, such as lettuce and spinach, which go to seed within weeks of being sown. Being biennial, chard doesn't set seed until its second year.

'Perpetual' (also listed as Perpetual Spinach) is one of the few varieties of cutting chard. Its leaves grow larger than those of spinach, are less acidic and lighter green. 'Ruby' and 'Paros', two good Swiss types, will lend color to any salad. 'Ruby' has dark green leaves, deeply veined in reddish purple; 'Paros', a French cultivar, has crisp white stems and crinkled dark green leaves.

New Zealand Spinach (*Tetragonia tetragonioides*) **and Malabar Spinach** (*Basella alba*)
While two warm-weather greens—New Zealand spinach and Malabar spinach—have "spinach" in their common names and a spinachlike flavor and texture, most greens lovers would quickly distinguish these pseudospinaches from the real thing. Slower to bolt than the genuine article and fine additions to the salad bowl, they're still worth growing, however.

New Zealand spinach continues to spread like a vine through both heat and

MESCLUN

Don't let its popularity in trendy restaurants discourage you from growing mesclun, a mix of leaf vegetables. The traditional ingredients are
arugula, curly endive, cutting chicory, dandelion and broadleaf cress,
but follow your own lights. Add lettuces, chervil, sorrel, chives and
purslane, anything you think will taste good in a salad. The secret of
mesclun is not its make-up but its harvest: Begin cutting as soon as the
plants are 2 inches tall, and never let any plant grow beyond 6 inches.

drought. The pointed, bright green leaves taste best when they are less than 2
inches long. Pinch off the young tip growth and you will not only fill your harvest
basket but also encourage new shoots to form. Like parsley, New Zealand
spinach seeds are slow to germinate, so I soak them overnight before sowing. I

Chard not only flourishes through the heat of summer, but in many parts of the country it also will endure considerable cold, thereby providing a harvest over many months. Two chards are pictured at left: one with red and the other with green petioles.

begin this green indoors, setting out seedlings two weeks after the last expected frost. I could sow a second crop directly in the garden at that time, but three plants are plenty for an ongoing contribution to most summer salads.

Malabar, or Indian, spinach also thrives in torrid conditions but wilts at the mention of frost. Its seeds, too, are slow to germinate, and gardeners north of USDA Zone 7 should start plants indoors, setting them outside about two weeks after the frost-free date. A vigorous climber, Malabar spinach easily reaches 4 feet on a trellis and makes an expedient replacement for peas that have run their course. Three plants, spaced about one foot apart, are plenty for most families. There is a red species, *B. rubra*, with attractive red stems and red-tinged leaves which is similar in growth to the green. Both should be harvested when their leaves reach 2 inches across, about eight weeks after planting.

Orach (*Atriplex hortensis*)

More colorful and taller than Malabar spinach is an annual green called orach, a domesticated relative of lamb's quarters (*Chenopodium album*) that thrives in alkaline soil. The red- and green-leafed forms are most common, but there are also magenta and yellow types. Most growers concur that the green type, sometimes called mountain spinach or sea purslane, is the sweetest-tasting orach.

All types can be seeded outdoors (sow 1/2 inch deep) from four to six weeks before the last frost, or as soon as the ground can be worked. Thin plants to one foot and begin harvesting at six weeks, either by picking the small leaves or by pulling the entire plant. If left uncut, orach will grow to more than 6 feet and put out long, intriguing flower spikes. To keep the salad bowl filled, pinch back any spikes as soon as they appear, and keep the plants to under 3 feet tall.

Leaf Amaranths (*Amaranthus* spp.)

Also known as hinn choy and Chinese spinach, leaf amaranth makes a good salad staple if you have a penchant for strong-flavored greens. The taste is sometimes described as nutty, but it is a nuttiness laced with horseradish. Tampala (*A. tricolor*) is perhaps the most widely cultivated of the leaf amaranths for greens. 'Joseph's Coat', a cultivar of *A. tricolor*, is more celebrated as an ornamental, but its leaves are perfectly edible and, like those of its relatives, are high in iron and vitamins A and C. A green form of love-lies-bleeding (*A. caudatus*) is also grown for the salad bowl.

There is little correlation between leaf color and flavor, but amaranths with oval leaves are a little sweeter and more succulent than those with narrow leaves. Many catalogs do not indicate botanical names for amaranths, but they do describe the foliage.

I sow seeds outdoors, 1/2 inch deep, after the danger of frost has passed. As the plants mature—some grow as tall as 5 feet—I thin them to 8 inches. Amaranths need plenty of water and are ready to harvest in about five weeks. One or two plants are plenty for most families.

With salads, adventurous spirits will be rewarded with a complexity of flavors.

Brassicas

Several members of *Brassica*, in the mustard family, thrive in warm weather to lend their distinctive flavors to any salad. Dwarf bok-choy (*Brassica rapa*, Chinensis group), sold under the varietal name 'Mei Qing Choi', has delicate light green leaves, with thick crisp ribs that are reminiscent of celery. In the hottest weather, the leaves take on a slight bitterness, but rarely do they become unpalatable. Sow seeds 1/2 inch deep a week or two before the last frost and thin young plants to every 6 to 8 inches. Leaves are ready to harvest, a few at a time from each plant, in about six weeks.

Mizuna is another wonderful accent plant, in part because of its light green, feathery foliage. Also known as Kyo-Na, this mustard germinates and grows quickly. It is better to harvest it sparingly until plants have developed a thick, full crown. Seeds should be sown only 1/4 inch deep two to four weeks before the frost-free date.

Kale (*B. oleracea,* Acephala group) is a mustard relative with the distinction of being our most nutritious cultivated green, offering 30 times more vitamin A and C than the crisphead lettuces. It is tolerant of both heat and cold, enduring the worst of summer in many parts of the country and then perking up with the approach of fall; a light frost sweetens its somewhat nutty flavor. Kale easily survives winter without protection as far north as Zone 6 (and even into Zone 5 with a bit of cover), and so provides fresh greens when most other crops have expired. Because its mature leaves are tough, kale is too often overlooked as a salad ingredient, but leaves picked when they are about 4 inches long are flavorful and tender.

'Red Russian' is an old, colorful variety with deeply lobed leaves that become russet when touched by frost. Another standard, 'Dwarf Blue Curled Vates', has shorter stems and is about one foot tall, compared with 2-foot 'Red Russian'. A new Dutch hybrid named 'Winterbor' sends up great "fronds" of bluish green, almost 3 feet tall. It is handsome and good flavored.

The greens mentioned here are enough to fill most salad bowls, but they don't exhaust the possibilities.

OTHER GREENS FOR THE SALAD

Corn salad, *Valerianella locusta*

Dandelion, *Taraxacum officinale*

Endive, *Cichorium endivia*

Garden cress, *Lepidium sativum*

Miner's lettuce, *Montia perfoliata*

Purslane, *Portulaca oleracea*

Upland cress, *Barbarea verna*

Watercress, *Nasturtium officinale*

Once you begin tossing some of these less widely appreciated leaves together, you may want to explore others. Gradually, the proportion of lettuce in your salads may diminish. You may even experience a horticultural and culinary revelation: lovely as lettuce is, you can make a wonderful salad without it. Q

A TOUCH OF COLOR
Tomatoes

BY CASS PETERSON

SLICED AND ACCOMPANIED by nothing but salt and pepper, or elegantly dressed and paired with herbs or greens, tomatoes (*Lycopersicon lycopersicum*) are the soul of summer salads. The standard red-fruited cultivars are still king in the garden, but tomatoes come in a palette of colors, from pale yellow to purple—even striped or marbled. Some produce pea-sized fruit, perfect for sprinkling atop mixed greens, while others produce two-pound lunkers that can be scooped out and used as edible salad bowls. While most of us prefer ripe tomatoes, green, unripe tomatoes also can be used to add tang to a salad (in fact, Italians prefer them that way, reserving ripe fruit for cooking).

The earliest tomatoes begin to ripen about seven weeks after they are set out and will continue to produce fruit until frost kills the plants. Although cultivars have been bred to accommodate a wide range of growing conditions, the tomato's basic requirements are relatively straightforward: It needs sun, warm temperatures, good but not overly rich soil and a steady supply of moisture.

The gardening season in most of temperate North America is too short to grow this heat-loving vegetable from a direct seeding in the soil, so you will need to start with a young plant. Whether purchased from a garden center or started in a pot on your own windowsill, the plant should be introduced gradually to outdoor conditions before it is transplanted into the garden. This "hardening off" process consists of putting the young plant outdoors during the day in a spot that is sunny but sheltered from the wind. Bring the plant in at night if frost threat-

Tomatoes come in a palette of colors, from pale yellow to purple—even striped or marbled.

A steady supply of moisture for growing tomatoes is very important. Water deeply once a week (unless there has been an inch of rain) and mulch the plants to reduce water loss. Middle: 'Sun Gold' cherry tomato is sweet and early. Bottom: 'Supersweet 100' cherry tomato is especially productive.

ens. A week or so of this treatment will toughen the tomato plant and help it thrive when it goes outside to stay.

Tomatoes will not withstand frost, so don't transplant until the soil has warmed to about 70° F and the nights are reliably above freezing. Some gardeners get a jump on the season by covering their young plants with clear plastic sheeting, spun polyester row covers, such as Reemay, or even old milk jugs. These techniques work well as long as only light frosts occur—perhaps a minimum of 29° F. If you do cover your tomatoes, be sure to remove or ventilate the covers on warm, sunny days to avoid overheating the plants.

When the weather is right and the young plant has hardened off, plant it as deeply as possible, so that the stem is buried and only the topmost leaves are above the soil surface. Additional roots will develop from the buried stem, further strengthening the plant. Tomatoes like moderate, steady fertility, the kind supplied by organic materials such as

Short-season gardeners often prefer determinate varieties, which ripen fruit more quickly than indeterminates, which provide a steadier supply all summer.

Large, naked, raw carrots are acceptable as food only to those who live in hutches eagerly awaiting Easter.

Fran Lebowitz,
Metropolitan Life, 1978

well-rotted manure or compost. Too much nitrogen all at once will result in lush plants with few fruits, so avoid or go easy on commercial fertilizers, especially those with a high N number in the NPK ratio that is printed on the bag.

A steady supply of moisture is also important. Tomatoes growing in soil that is either overly dry or water-logged will produce fruits with sunken, black lesions on the bottom. This condition, blossom-end rot, can be avoided by keeping the soil evenly

CANDIDATES FOR THE TOMATO PATCH

	DET/INDET	COLOR
EARLY VARIETIES (50-65 DAYS)		
'BELLSTAR'	D	RED
'BURPEE'S PIXIE'	D	RED
'EARLY GIRL'	I	RED
'EARLIROUGE'	D	RED
'FIRST LADY'	I	RED
'GOLD NUGGET'	D	GOLD
'LA ROMA'	D	RED
'ORANGE PIXIE'	D	ORANGE
'OREGON SPRING'	D	RED
'PILGRIM'	D	RED
'RED CURRANT'	I	RED
'SIBERIA'	D	RED
'STUPICE'	I	RED
'SUN GOLD'	I	GOLD
'SUPER CHIEF'	D	RED
'TIGERELLA'	I	ORANGE/YELLOW
'WHIPPERSNAPPER'	D	DARK PINK
'YELLOW CURRANT'	I	YELLOW
	KEY:	D=DETERMINATE; I=INDETERMINATE;

moist. Water deeply once a week (unless the week has produced at least an inch of rain) and mulch the plants with straw or compost to reduce water loss.

Most tomato cultivars are vining plants and will flop over and trail across the ground as they grow. Letting the plant sprawl won't hurt fruit production, but the fruits will be cleaner, easier to pick and less likely to be damaged by insects or molds if you provide some support for the vine. Tomato cages—essentially cylinders of fence wire—are a simple and popular means of supporting tomato plants, though many are too small and flimsy to handle a large plant. Be sure to install the cage over the plant while it is still small enough to fit inside easily. You can also drive a stake next to the young plant and tie the vine to the stake with strips of cloth as it grows. Staking or caging also improves air circulation around the plant, which helps avoid the fungal diseases to which tomatoes are susceptible.

Excessive rain and high humidity also invite disease. If wet conditions are the norm in your garden, look for tomato varieties that offer high disease resistance,

TYPE	COMMENTS
P	LARGE PLUM TYPE
C	16-INCH PLANTS
S	VERY EARLY CROP
S	SETS FRUITS IN EXTREME TEMPERATURES
S	GOOD DISEASE RESISTANCE
C	NEARLY SEEDLESS
P	HEAVY YIELDS
C	1-TO-2-INCH FRUITS
S	ADAPTED TO COOL REGIONS
S	COMPACT PLANTS; EXCELLENT FLAVOR
C	SMALL, WILD CURRANT SPECIES
S	SETS FRUITS IN EXTREME COLD; VERY SMALL PLANTS
S	HEIRLOOM; ADAPTED TO COOL, SHORT SEASONS; COMPACT
C	SWEET AND EARLY
S	VERY EARLY; LARGE FRUITS
S	TANGY FLAVOR
C	EXTRA EARLY
C	VERY SMALL, WILD CURRANT SPECIES
S=SLICING TOMATO; C=CHERRY TOMATO; P=PROCESSING/PLUM TOMATO	

such as 'Big Beef' or 'Celebrity', both large, red-fruited varieties. Insect pests are usually not serious, but some gardeners are troubled with tomato hornworms (large, pale green caterpillars) or Colorado potato beetles. Both are large, so you can pick them off the plant and crush them.

WHAT TO GROW

Determinate or Indeterminate? Tomatoes are typically designated "inde-terminate" or "determinate" in seed catalogues. Indeterminate varieties grow, bloom and ripen fruit as long as the weather permits; if the growing season is long enough, they can become very large plants, 12 feet and taller. Determinate varieties are more compact, generally growing only a few feet tall. They tend to bloom and set most of their fruit all at once.

Short-season gardeners often prefer determinates, which ripen fruit more

Right: Many heirloom and modern hybrid tomatoes are large—with fruits starting at 8 ounces and running up to 2 pounds or more. Tiny cherry tomatoes can be served whole or halved.

	DET/INDET	COLOR
MID-SEASON VARIETIES (65-80 DAYS)		
'ACE-HY'	D	RED
'ARKANSAS TRAVELER'	I	PINK
'BETTER BOY'	I	RED
'BLACK PRINCE'	I	DARK RED
'BRANDYWINE'	I	PINK/RED
'CHEROKEE PURPLE'	I	PINK/PURPLE
'DUTCHMAN'	I	DARK PINK
'ENTERPRISE'	D	RED
'EVERGREEN'	I	GREEN
'HAWAIIAN'	I	RED
'HEAT WAVE'	D	RED
'HEINZ 1350'	D	RED
'HUSKY GOLD'	I	GOLD
'JET STAR'	I	RED
'LEMON BOY'	I	YELLOW
'PARKS OG 50 WHOPPER'	I	RED
	KEY: D=DETERMINATE; I=INDETERMINATE;

TYPE	COMMENTS
S	ADAPTED TO CALIFORNIA
S	SOUTHERN HEIRLOOM
S	GOOD DISEASE RESISTANCE
S	COMPACT VINE; VERY TASTY AND JUICY
S	AMISH HEIRLOOM; SUPERB FLAVOR
S	MULTICOLOR FLESH; SOUTHERN HEIRLOOM
S	LOW-ACID BEEFSTEAK
S	EXCELLENT DISEASE RESISTANCE
S	GREEN FLESH; MILD FLAVOR
S	HEAT TOLERANT
S	HEAT TOLERANT
P	CANNING VARIETY
S	DWARF INDETERMINATE
S	EXCELLENT FLAVOR, LOW ACID
S	WIDELY ADAPTED; MILD FLAVOR
S	GOOD DISEASE RESISTANCE

S=SLICING TOMATO; C=CHERRY TOMATO; P=PROCESSING/PLUM TOMATO

quickly than indeterminates. Many gardeners with long seasons like to plant at least one determinate variety to hasten the tomato harvest. Indeterminates, in contrast, provide a steadier supply of fresh tomatoes for the table all summer.

Among the standard, red-fruited tomatoes, 'Better Boy' and 'Park's OG 50 Whopper' are indeterminates that have grown well in gardens throughout the country. Another old favorite is 'Early Girl', an indeterminate that starts ripening its small, sweet-tart fruits just eight weeks after transplanting. The determinate 'Oregon Spring' is especially good in the Pacific Northwest, where cool spring temperatures often hamper fruit set. Gardeners in the South and Southwest, where excessive heat is sometimes troublesome, should consider 'Solarset' or 'Heat Wave', disease-resistant indeterminates bred to tolerate high temperatures.

Tomatoes of a Different Color. If you're tired of seeing red, there are exciting possibilities in tomatoes of a different color. A few modern hybrids are worthwhile, especially 'Lemon Boy', an indeterminate that produces large and tasty pale yellow fruits. But the best color range is to be found in the category of open-pollinated heirloom tomatoes, varieties handed down by generations of gardeners. Many of these tomatoes are too perishable to interest commercial growers,

	DET/INDET	COLOR
MID-SEASON VARIETIES (65-80 DAYS)		
'QUICK PICK'	I	RED
'ROMA'	D	RED
'RUTGERS'	D	RED
'SMALL FRY'	D	RED
'SOLARSET'	D	RED
SUNNY'	D	RED
'SUPERSONIC'	D	RED
'SUPERSWEET 100'	I	RED
'SWEET MILLION'	I	RED
'SWEET 100'	I	RED
'THE JUICE'	D	RED
'VALENCIA'	I	ORANGE
'VEEPICK'	D	RED
'WHITE BEAUTY'	I	WHITE
'YELLOW PEAR'	I	YELLOW
	KEY:	D=DETERMINATE; I=INDETERMINATE;

but their superior taste and interesting colors make them well worth space in the home salad garden.

'Cherokee Purple' is soft-fleshed and fragile, but the flavor is superb and the dusky purple-magenta color arresting; 'Tangerine' is large and vividly orange; 'Black Prince' (really sort of an olive brown) is smooth, firm and flavorful; the mild 'White Beauty' is spectacular layered on a salad plate with 'Evergreen', which ripens amber green with emerald green flesh. 'Tigerella' bears one-inch fruits striped red and yellow, and 'Pineapple' produces huge fruits with golden flesh marbled in red. Among the best flavored of the heirlooms are the pink-skinned beefsteak types, including 'Giant Belgium', 'Brandywine' and 'Dutchman'.

Cherry Tomatoes. Many heirlooms and modern hybrid tomatoes are on the large end of the size scale, with fruits starting at eight ounces and running up to two pounds or more. But small tomatoes—including cherry tomatoes, which can be served whole or halved—are excellent candidates for the salad garden. Bear in mind that many cherry tomatoes are large, viny indeterminate plants that produce prolifically. A plant or two will produce enough fruit to supply the average family for a season. Among the best are 'Supersweet 100', which produces small

TYPE	COMMENTS
S	HEAVY YIELDS; HIGH QUALITY
C	STANDARD PASTE VARIETY
P	CANNING FAVORITE
C	HEAVY YIELDS; COMPACT PLANTS
S	HEAT TOLERANT
S	SOUTHERN COMMERCIAL VARIETY
S	ALL-AROUND PERFORMER
C	SWEET AND PRODUCTIVE
C	IMPROVED VERSION OF 'SWEET 100'
C	HUGE YIELDS; RAMPANT VINES
P	FOR CANNING OR JUICE
S	MAINE HEIRLOOM
P	PLUM; PEELS EASILY
S	MILD AND SWEET
C	HEIRLOOM; MILD FLAVOR

S=SLICING TOMATO; C=CHERRY TOMATO; P=PROCESSING/PLUM TOMATO

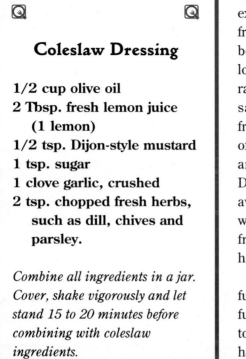

Coleslaw Dressing

1/2 cup olive oil
2 Tbsp. fresh lemon juice
   (1 lemon)
1/2 tsp. Dijon-style mustard
1 tsp. sugar
1 clove garlic, crushed
2 tsp. chopped fresh herbs,
   such as dill, chives and
   parsley.

Combine all ingredients in a jar. Cover, shake vigorously and let stand 15 to 20 minutes before combining with coleslaw ingredients.

crimson fruits; 'Sungold', which has exceptionally sweet tangerine-colored fruits; and 'Yellow Pear', an heirloom bearing mild-flavored tomatoes that look like miniature pears. 'Red Currant' and 'Yellow Currant' are also fine salad tomatoes, bearing their tiny fruits in grape-like clusters. Because of their diminutive size, these are also among the first tomatoes to ripen. Determinate cherry tomatoes also are available, including 'Gold Nugget', which produces loads of mild, yellow fruits, and 'Whippersnapper', which has firm, pink fruits.

Tomatoes are at their best picked fully ripe, when they have developed full color and are slightly soft to the touch. But they also can be harvested half ripe and allowed to ripen fully on a countertop, undisturbed and out of direct sun. When frost threatens, pick any tomato that shows a hint of color and wrap in tissue or newspaper to finish ripening. Immature green tomatoes won't ripen, but they can still be sliced thinly and enjoyed in a salad, Italian style.

	DET/INDET	COLOR
LATE-SEASON VARIETIES (80+ DAYS)		
'CAL-ACE'	D	RED
'GIANT BELGIUM'	I	DARK PINK
'GOLDEN BOY'	I	YELLOW
'HOMESTEAD 24-F'	D	RED
'PINEAPPLE'	I	RED/YELLOW
'SAN MARZANO'	I	RED
'SUPER BUSH'	D	RED
'TANGERINE'	I	YELLOW/ORANGE
	KEY:	D=DETERMINATE; I=INDETERMINATE;

'Brandywine' is an Amish heirloom with superb flavor.

TYPE	COMMENTS
S	ADAPTED TO ARID AREAS
S	LOW ACID; VERY LARGE
S	MILD FLAVOR
S	ADAPTED TO THE SOUTH
S	STRIPED HEIRLOOM
P	MILD, MEATY; PASTE TYPE
S	REQUIRES NO SUPPORT
S	HEIRLOOM BEEFSTEAK
S=SLICING TOMATO; C=CHERRY TOMATO; P=PROCESSING/PLUM TOMATO	

OTHER VEGETABLES
The Rest of the Salad

BY PAUL DUNPHY

T HE SALAD BOWL is a mirror of the gardening season. Within its smooth curve is captured the arrival of each herb and vegetable at a ripe and tender stage. Almost every plant we cultivate, and many that grow wild, can be artfully blended in the salad bowl. Uncooked beans, Jerusalem artichokes and summer squash are superb salad ingredients. What follows are sketches of some of my favorite vegetables, other than leafy greens, that can be used raw in salads. They are versatile and easy to grow. They are the rest of the salad.

'Packman' broccoli

Broccoli (*Brassica oleracea*, Botrytis group)

Folk wisdom and scientific knowledge have found common ground in broccoli plants. Recent research has affirmed long-standing parental assertations that broccoli is, indeed, "good for you." Harvested when the heads are small, uncooked broccoli is a superb addition to a salad. Added to its established health and culinary merits is this horticultural distinction: Broccoli is one of the most productive plants in the salad garden. Three- or four-week-old seedlings set out 16 inches apart 10 days before the last expected frost will begin producing harvestable-sized heads in less than two months. In many parts of the country, the plants will continue to send out smaller side shoots for three or four months.

Broccoli requires soil rich in nitrogen—aged manure is a good source—and close to a neutral pH (7.0). It does best in cool, moist conditions and temperatures between 40° and 65° F, and likes plenty of water, at least one inch per week. In regions with fiercely hot summers, an early season crop will languish. Uncut heads bolt, or go to seed; however, a second crop, planted toward the end

Carrots, daikon radishes and beets make a beautiful, unusual salad without the greens.

of summer, will begin yielding in fall. Only Saharan heat or Arctic cold will put an end to broccoli's productivity.

Broccoli can be grouped in three categories. Calabrese types, the most common commercial broccolis, have been bred to produce one large dome-shaped central head. Salad growers should choose Calabrese cultivars that bear a bounty of side shoots long after the main head has been cut, such as 'Packman', 'Emperor', 'Green Comet' and 'Umpqua Dark Green'. Romanesco-type broccolis produce a spiral of florets on a conical head. The Romanesco 'Minaret' has chartreuse heads; others bear heads of bright apple-green. Plants of the third category, sprouting broccoli, send up small loose heads colored either purple or white. Sprouting types, such as 'Purple Sprouting' and 'White Sprouting', are long-season broccolis, taking four months or more to mature. In mild climates, they can be planted in fall for spring harvest.

'Midway' cabbage

Cabbage (*Brassica oleracea*, Capitata group)

Well-chosen varieties of cabbage have a crispness, nutritional value and elegant color that elevates this vegetable above its unfairly pedestrian reputation. Entire salads and slaws can be made from only a portion of a single head. What isn't used can be stored for many days in the refrigerator. Given its keeping quality and culinary contributions, even gardeners with postage-stamp plots should consider making space for a least two or three heads of cabbage.

Space is the primary challenge to raising cabbage. Growing just one large head can take nearly 6 square feet. Fortunately, several small heads are better than one large head for fresh salads. Short-season types, such as the heirloom 'Early Jersey Wakefield' or the hybrids 'Elisa' and 'Minicole' require far less space and can be set about 12 inches apart. Most reach a harvestable size of one to two pounds within two months of being transplanted into the garden. 'Salarite', a small loose-headed variety, has especially good flavor. Red varieties, such as 'Ruby Perfection' or the flamboyant 'Scarlett O'Hara', or savoy types, such as

'Savoy Ace', 'Spivoy' and 'Promasa Baby' also can be grown at a 12-inch spacing. Their heads may be smaller than those of giants like 'Wisconsin All Seasons' and 'Tropic Giant', but they are better suited for home gardens and for fresh dishes. Interestingly, crowding plants appears to increase their "cabbagey" flavor.

Like most members of the mustard family, cabbage is cold tolerant. Early varieties are usually seeded indoors, then set out two or three weeks before the last expected frost. I like to sow a second crop in midsummer, which will mature in late fall. In mild regions of the country, gardeners can plant cabbage in fall and harvest in spring. Humus-rich loam is ideal for growing cabbages, which have a fairly shallow fibrous root system. I apply a mulch of compost to keep the roots cool and help maintain moisture; cabbages that have been water stressed often have a strong off-flavor.

Several insects trouble cabbage, but only cutworms pose a serious threat. A cardboard collar around each transplant is good protection in soils that harbor cutworms. Other insects may disfigure a few leaves, but given plenty of water and relatively cool temperatures, cabbage plants will grow vigorously until you deem them firm and ready to harvest. Cut the head an inch or two above the ground, and the plant may sprout new leaves for still another dish of coleslaw.

Carrots need light, fertile, well-drained soil.

Carrots (*Daucus carota* ssp. *sativus*)

Patience is one of the great virtues of the carrot. Unlike broccoli, say, or cauliflower, carrots do not tumble from a peak of ripeness to an inedible state in a matter of days. Pull a few carrots today and they may be wonderful. Pull a few more next week and they will be just as sweet.

"Baby" carrots are some of the best for salads. 'Little Finger', 'Amsterdam Forcing', 'Lady Finger', 'Minicor' and 'Mokum' all produce sweet, dark orange roots only 3 or 4 inches long. Paris market types, such as 'Planet', 'Thumbelina', 'Parmex' and 'Parisier', form spheres slightly smaller than a golf ball, but they can be harvested while still the size of a marble. The long, blunt-ended Nantes carrots, varieties such as 'Rondino', 'Napoli' and 'Touchon', are the most versatile. 'A-Plus', a super-sweet hybrid with a higher content of carotene and vitamin A, is another fine variety. All these carrots can be harvested early, when only 1/2 inch across the shoulder, or late in the season when they are three or four times as broad. Young or old, they are crisp and sweet.

Carrots demand light soil that is fertile and water retentive yet well draining. It must be well-tilled—roots encountering even a small stone will fork or become misshapen. A pH between 6.0 and 6.5 is perfect for carrots, and the soil should be rich in potassium and phosphorus. Too much nitrogen also produces misshapen roots covered with an excess of tiny feeder roots. Tolerant of cold, carrots can be direct seeded in the garden at least a month before the last frost; plants grow best in temperatures between 60° and 65° F.

Try to sow the seeds about 1/2 inch apart, in rows every 6 inches, and thin the little plants by snipping off their tops as soon as they become entwined. A second and third thinning may be needed, but by the time you make your way down the rows the third time, pull rather than cut the plants, for they should be large enough to become salad material.

Orange cauliflower

Cauliflower (*Brassica oleracea*, Botrytis group)

Most salad lovers appreciate the mild flavor and delicate texture of cauliflower. Its white heads, or curds, offer a striking visual contrast to the red of tomatoes, orange of carrots and green of lettuce in a garden salad. Unfortunately, cauliflower is often viewed as a time-consuming and finicky plant to grow. It is less tolerant of frost than cabbage, and so cannot be set out as early, and is even more unhappy in heat. For many varieties to produce firm, white curds, gardeners must tie the outer leaves up, around the curd, as soon as the center starts to form.

In practice, though, raising cauliflower is less demanding and more rewarding than it sounds. Rich soil and attentive watering will carry plants through hot spells (there are also cultivars, such as 'Andes', 'Stovepipe' and 'Hormade' that are more heat tolerant). You can eliminate the need for binding up leaves by choosing self-blanching, or self-wrapping, varieties whose foliage naturally curls around the head, such as the open-pollinated varieties 'Self Blanche' and 'Alert', or modern hybrids, such as 'Avalanche'.

Another alternative is to grow one of the purple strains of cauliflower, which don't need to be blanched, such as 'Violet Queen' or 'Purple Giant'. 'Violet Queen' has the added quality of setting

> **Cauliflower is nothing but cabbage with a college education.**
>
> Mark Twain,
> *Pudd'nhead Wilson*, 1894.

sideshoots after the main head has been cut. Few other cauliflowers produce shoots, so their productivity per plant is limited, and each curd is precious. To get the most from your plants, don't let a single head go by. Harvest blanching types before the heads begin to segment or develop a purple blush, which is an indication of stress.

Cauliflower can be started indoors a month before the last expected frost, then set out around the frost-free date. Space plants 18 to 20 inches apart and give them the same care you would broccoli or cabbage, but a bit more of it. The reward is a generous harvest of what many gardeners consider the "queen of the brassicas."

Bush-type 'Kirby' cucumbers

Cucumbers (*Cucumis sativus*)

Cucumbers can make a small garden seem larger. The vining types—as opposed to the bush types—are willing climbers. They can be trained to poles or a trellis and will bear an abundance of fruit in a relatively small space. They do not twine as beans do, so they must be tied and guided when grown on a pole, but on a trellis, their tendrils will grab as they climb. Let the central leader grow to the top of the trellis, then pinch it off to encourage lateral growth.

Trellised cukes not only make more efficient use of space than plants allowed to ramble across the ground, they produce more and straighter fruit. There are scores of varieties to choose from, but some of the best for salads are 'Orient Express', 'Sweet Success', 'Streamliner' and 'Early Pride', as well as the Middle Eastern cultivars 'Kidma' and 'Sweet Alphee'. If you prefer bush types, try 'Salad Bush', an All-America Selections winner, or 'Bush Champion'. Gardeners with plenty of space who want to grow something different should try 'True Lemon', an oval yellow cucumber that may have visitors to the garden guessing about its identity.

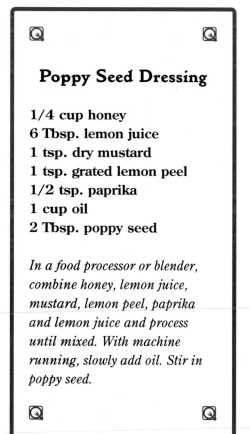

Poppy Seed Dressing

1/4 cup honey
6 Tbsp. lemon juice
1 tsp. dry mustard
1 tsp. grated lemon peel
1/2 tsp. paprika
1 cup oil
2 Tbsp. poppy seed

In a food processor or blender, combine honey, lemon juice, mustard, lemon peel, paprika and lemon juice and process until mixed. With machine running, slowly add oil. Stir in poppy seed.

Don't be misled by seed catalogues that label some varieties as cornichons, those finger-sized cucumbers that supermarkets sell for exorbitant prices. Although some breeders have developed "cornichon" varieties, cornichons are nothing more than small cucumbers. Harvest early and your 'Sweet Success' becomes a cornichon. Above all, keep harvesting: Cucumbers grow rapidly and unpicked plants will cease to set fruits.

Natives of India, cucumbers thrive in warmth. For an early harvest, begin plants indoors (about two weeks before the frost-free date). Thin to one plant per pot and set them out, one foot apart, a week after the risk of frost has passed. Choose a garden location with good air circulation and drainage—I like to rake the soil up 6 to 8 inches to create an elevated bed or hill—and be sure the soil is enriched with organic matter and has a nearly neutral pH (7.0). Cucumbers are greedy feeders. If you choose to protect your plants from cucumber beetles and other insects with floating row covers, be sure to remove them when the first flowers appear, since cucumbers are pollinated by bees.

'Cascadia' sugar snap pea

Peas (*Pisum sativum*)

Peas are one of the oldest cultivated vegetables—Thomas Jefferson was growing more than 50 varieties 200 years ago—yet they are an underused addition to the salad bowl. All types—garden peas, snow peas and snap peas—require the same conditions in the garden: full sun and well-drained soil with a pH between 6.0 and 7.0. Because peas, like other legumes, can obtain nitrogen by way of bacteria that form on their roots, they don't require exceptionally rich soil, especially nitrogen-rich soil. You can boost the nitrogen-fixing process by moistening the seeds and then dusting them with a beneficial bacterium, a gray powder called a legume innoculent which is sold in small quantities through many garden catalogs. The innoculant is less useful if you are planting in ground where peas have grown before, and where the bacteria is already present in the soil.

Peas love cool weather and can survive light freezes. They grow best when temperatures range between 55 and 70° F. Sow seeds one inch deep, tamping the row with your foot, as soon as the soil can be worked, up to six weeks before and until three weeks after the last frost. For an autumn crop, sow in late summer (most varieties require between 55 and 90 days to mature, so count back from the time of the first expected frost to determine the exact planting date), setting the seeds 2 or 3 inches deep to keep them from drying out and mulching the young plants to help keep the soil cool. Plants in rows should be thinned to about 4 inches apart. I plant tall varieties, such as the 5-foot heirloom 'Tall Telephone', in double rows, 8 inches apart, with a support running between them.

Despite seed-catalogue hyperbole about bush varieties, all peas do better when they have something to climb on. I like using light-weight plastic netting—it's simple to install and reusable—but any vertical guide will do as long as the plants' tendrils can cling to its surface. Don't delay putting up a trellis—trying to untangle 10-inch-long pea vines and guide them upward is a frustrating job.

With all the hoopla over snap peas in the last few years, it's easy to forget the merits of traditional garden types. 'Lincoln' is a classic variety, high yielding and high quality; 'Green Arrow' offers generous crops on shorter vines. 'Freezonian', a 1948 AAS winner, is still widely planted; 'Wando' is another reliable variety. Resistant to heat, it is a good choice for warm climates. 'Maestro' is known for producing many double pods and for its disease resistance; 'Waverex' is an outstanding *petit pois*, or baby pea, type.

'Carouby de Maussane', a 5-foot French heirloom, still sets the standard for snow, or edible-pod, peas. 'Short 'n Sweet', a compact cultivar, is ready in 50 days. 'Dwarf Gray Sugar' is the standard mid-season snow pea; 'Oregon Sugar Pod', is another widely adapted variety with added disease resistance. 'Snowbird' and 'Snowflake', ready in about 60 days, are ideal for short-season gardeners.

Snap (or sugar snap) peas, perhaps the most important "new" vegetable of the last 25 years, just keep multiplying. 'Sugar Snap' was the first, a 1979 AAS winner. Its offspring are many, including 'Sugar Ann', 'Sugar Bon', 'Sugar Daddy', 'Sugar Mel', 'Sugar Pop', 'Sugar Rae' and more. My favorites are two compact varieties, 'Sugar Bon', which is especially early, and 'Sugar Daddy', the first "stringless" snap pea.

Peas should be picked promptly—just when they've filled out the pods, for garden peas; just as the pea begins to enlarge, for snow peas; and while the pea is still small, for snap peas. Save the spent plants for the compost pile. Like corn, their sugars begin to convert to starch as soon as they are harvested, so use peas immediately.

Sweet bell peppers

Sweet Peppers (*Capsicum annuum*)

Sweet peppers mature in many colors, from lavender and purple to flame orange, yellow and chocolate brown. They can be eaten "green," of course, but it is for non-green hues we pay so dearly at the supermarket. For gardeners with cool abbreviated seasons, growing any sweet pepper is a challenge; waiting for a sweet pepper to change from green to a brighter color may be impossible. Don't let the days-to-maturity number in seed catalogues mislead you: The number refers to the

Sweet red peppers

time from transplanting outdoors to harvestable *green* peppers.

If your garden is cursed with a late spring and an early autumn, small varieties like 'Jingle Bells', have the best chance of fully ripening. Also worth trying are 'North Star', 'Merrimack Wonder', 'New Ace', 'Golden Summer', 'Sweet Chocolate' and 'Yankee', all of which should do well in northern regions. In areas with longer seasons, gardeners have the latitude to raise jumbo varieties like 'California Wonder' and 'Big Bertha'. Different from the familiar bell peppers are Italian types known as bull's horn peppers, because of their long curved shapes. 'Corno di Toro', 'Red Marconi' and 'Italia' are widely available varieties. Worth trying, too, are the Lamuyo-type peppers, which are larger and more elongated than bell varieties. One common name is 'Vidi'. And one last choice: 'Ivory Charm', a bell hybrid, which begins creamy white and ends soft yellow.

In most parts of the country, pepper seeds should be sown in pots at least eight weeks before the last expected frost. Young plants cannot be set out safely until two weeks after the frost-free date—even a hint of cold can stunt growth and cause blossoms to fall off. In addition to warmth, peppers require plenty of moisture (though their fibrous roots also demand good drainage), full sun and slightly acid soil rich in organic matter. Giving plants some protection from the cool breezes of early summer will encourage the growth of stocky plants capable of setting more than a dozen fruits. Once the season is winding down and many peppers are still small and green, remove the smallest and let the plant concentrate on those fruits with the best chance of ripening.

Radishes (*Raphanus sativus*)

In one way, radishes are an alter ego of the sweet pepper. Each lends crunch and color to salad, but not necessarily the color red. Like peppers, radishes ripen in a multitude of hues—purple, white, pale green, rose and red. But while peppers demand heat, radishes like it cool. While peppers are excruciatingly slow to ripen, radishes are explosively quick.

Spring varieties can be planted directly in the garden about a month before

Fresh from the spring garden—a scrumptious medley of peas, broccoli and edible blooms.

the frost-free date. Sow the seed 1/2 inch deep, two seeds per inch, and stand back: In a long row, the first seeds are almost sprouting by the time you reach the end. The radishes will be ready to thin (to 3 inches) in two weeks and ready to harvest two weeks after that. To have a constant supply of radishes until the onset of hot weather, plant a three-foot row every six days for four weeks. Radishes are a cool-weather crop. Once the weather heats up or becomes dry, they become woody and their flavor turns—first sharp, then bitter. Plants that have gone to seed aren't a complete loss, however: The small seed pods are a lively addition to salads.

Radishes like light, well-drained soil that has been heavily amended with humus or well-rotted manure. Don't overdo the nitrogen, which produces superb leaves and undersized roots, and keep the soil slightly acid (5.5 to 6.8). Be sure to provide an even supply of water: Roots that have been subjected to dry, then wet conditions are likely to crack.

'Saxa'—ready to pull in 20 days—is the variety to plant if you want to be first in your neighborhood to have fresh radishes. Its round root is smaller than old favorites like AAS winners 'Cherry Bell', 'Champion' and 'Comet'. 'Gala' and 'Roodbol' are two other fine varieties. 'Valentine', also a round radish, has a surprise inside: reddish flesh. But globe-shaped radishes are only one part of the story. There are cylindrical varieties, such as 'Flamboyant' and 'Fluo', that are known as "French breakfast" radishes. Colored red with a white tip, they grow 3 or 4 inches long. Also popular are white radishes, varieties like 'White Icicle', which is elongated, and round types, such as 'Hailstone', 'Snow Belle' and 'White Globe'. 'Pink Beauty' is an unusual rose-pink color; 'Purple Plum' has bright purple skin; and the 4-inch root of 'French Golden' is light gold. Gardeners who don't want to buy several packets of seeds should try 'Easter Egg', a hybrid mix that produces white, red, purple, pink and violet radishes.

Most daikon, or Japanese, radishes are white and large—12 inches and longer. A familiar ingredient in Asian stir-fries, they can be peeled and thinly sliced and used uncooked in salads. 'Omny', 'Tokinashi', and 'April Cross' are well-known varieties. Unlike spring radishes such as 'Cherry Bell', daikon varieties take from 50 to 80 days to form mature roots.

Turnips (*Brassica rapa*, Rapifera group)
While turnip greens are often tossed in salads, too few gardeners take advantage of the turnip root. Peeled and thinly sliced, uncooked turnip is a first-rate addition to the salad bowl. Its crisp texture and mild flavor are two reasons why turnips should not be relegated to the stewpot.

Like most of its cousins in the mustard family, turnips flourish in cool temperatures. In the north, they are typically planted in early spring, as soon as the ground can be worked, for harvesting 35 to 50 days later; gardeners in warmer parts of the country sow seeds in autumn and pull their crop in spring. Spring or fall, turnips must grow quickly in temperatures around 60° F or they will become woody and bitter tasting.

For salad use, be sure to choose a mild variety, such as 'Rouge de Nancy', an early globe-shaped bicolor, or 'Just Right', a white-skinned globe-shaped hybrid that was an All-America Selections winner in 1960. 'Market Express' is another white hybrid, an especially sweet variety.

Organically rich, slightly acid soil is ideal for turnips, which should be spaced about 6 inches apart (the tender thinnings make fine salad greens). It's a good idea to mulch, both to retain moisture and to keep the soil cool, but don't fertilize: Overly rich soil will yield hefty leaves and undersized roots. Turnips are always best when they're harvested young and succulent, no more than 3 inches in diameter.

SALADS FOR
LANDLESS GARDENERS
Growing in Containers

BY SYDNEY EDDISON

Q

A FEW YEARS AGO, advancing age and a shrinking household gave me the excuse to turn a large vegetable garden back to lawn. Before long, however, I discovered that while local produce stands furnished sweet corn superior to mine, there was no substitute for home-grown tomatoes and lettuce covered with the morning's dew. Most of all I missed green beans— thin, elegant French beans, generically called *haricots verts*, which taste delicious in a mustard vinaigrette dressing.

Thus, I came to container salad gardening. Now, instead of bending double and slogging down a 50-foot row of beans, I perch on the low brick wall surrounding our terrace and harvest handfuls of 'Astrelle', our favorite bean, from a plastic pot 2 feet in diameter and 8 inches deep. In addition to beans, I grow lettuces, tomatoes, peppers, carrots, cucumbers, radishes, Swiss chard and many different herbs in pots and whiskey barrels.

While I arrived at my kitchen-garden-on-the-terrace by choice, other vegetable growers have had container gardening thrust upon them. Tamara Sellman is such a gardener. This dauntless young woman and her husband built a 14-by-20-foot-long deck at the back of their suburban Chicago townhouse. There, she grows everything in containers, from salad greens to herbs to hot-blooded chilies. Her footed plastic containers measure 18 by 30 by approximately 20 inches deep, and are durable enough to withstand the rigors of the midwestern climate and big enough to support a cornucopia of vegetables.

Adventurous and upbeat, Sellman makes clear that a 100 square-foot plot isn't necessary for salad gardening. She grows 'Greek Miniature' basil, which "looks like green topiary," and 'Little Gem' lettuce, a hybrid that takes up a minimum of space; pronounces Italian flat-leaf parsley "a fabulous tub plant" and likes arugula because "you can keep cutting it back"—a technique that works with many greens. She encourages tub gardeners to try some of the other specialty greens that have done particularly well on her deck, including cultivated purslane, radicchio, New Zealand spinach and sorrel. She's enthusiastic about cucumbers like 'Spacemaster', which produce full-sized fruits on short 3-foot vines. And if you want a real triumph, she recommends planting a tomatillo (*Physalis ixocarpa*).

Beans, lettuces, tomatoes, carrots, cucumbers, radishes, chards and much more can be grown successfully in containers.

Weeding around vegetables grown in containers or raised beds is nearly optional.

This Latin American vegetable yields 2-inch yellow fruits inside papery husks that look like Chinese lanterns.

"I grew one that was 5 feet tall," she says gleefully. "And now I have so many tomatillos that I couldn't possibly eat them all. You can eat them raw or poached, or you can make green salsa with them." In addition to growing vegetables, Sellman publishes *Cachepot: The Container Vegetable Gardener's Companion* (see Further Reading, page 104), which captures its creator's enthusiasm and offers valuable first-hand advice for those who want or must raise food crops in contained spaces.

Nona Koivula, Executive Director of All-America Selections, is also a container gardener. Her organization, which serves home gardeners by identifying the best in seed-grown flowers and vegetables each year, has singled out many salad vegetables as good candidates for tub culture. The 1994 AAS award-winning cucumber 'Fanfare' is one; it is a compact vine and is disease- and stress-resistant. 'Salad Bush', a 1988 AAS-winning cucumber, is another fine variety for containers. A pepper called 'Gypsy' won the approval of AAS in 1981 and flourishes in containers. Koivula also recommends 'Small Fry' tomato, a 1970 AAS winner, but points out that most tomatoes are adaptable to container growing. Bushlike determinate types are better candidates for pots and tubs because their terminal buds set fruit after reaching 2 or 3 feet, instead of continuing to grow onward and upward like their indeterminate relations.

Suitable tomatoes for containers are legion: 'Gem State', a determinate type with small red fruits developed for the northern Rocky Mountain region; 'Husky Gold', with delicious five-ounce yellow fruits; 'Whippersnapper' and 'Tumbler', cherry tomatoes especially bred for hanging baskets; and two tiny varieties that can be grown in 6-inch pots, 'Red Robin' and 'Yellow Canary', with red and yellow fruits, respectively. Joe Seals, the horticulturist at Park Seed Company in South Carolina, warns that these tiny tomatoes are "cute but not very productive. You probably wouldn't get more than a dozen tomatoes from each plant." For serious eating, he favors 'Better Bush Improved', which has 4-inch fruits on compact plants with handsome foliage. There is also a cherry version of 'Better Bush Improved'

Celery Seed Dressing

1 clove garlic
1/2 cup sugar
1 tsp. dry mustard
1 tsp. celery seed
1/2 tsp. paprika
3/4 cup oil
1/3 cup honey
1/3 cup vinegar
2 Tbsp. fresh lemon juice
Salt and freshly ground pepper

In a food processor, mince garlic. Add sugar, mustard, celery seed and paprika. Pulse, just to mix. With the processor running, add oil, honey, vinegar and lemon juice. Process until blended. Salt and pepper to taste.

Place containers where they will get plenty of sun, but remember that soil in pots dries out faster than soil in the garden.

that does splendidly when grown in a container.

Growing tomatoes and other salad vegetables in containers is nearly as easy as growing them in the garden. One tomato or several leafy vegetables require at least a three-gallon container (24 inches deep), though five gallons is far better; a single herb plant can be grown in a smaller pot. All containers should have bottom holes for drainage and be heavy enough so that they won't overturn. If your crop requires trellising, be sure to provide good support. That's difficult in a single pot, so I locate containers that will hold climbing plants, such as cucumbers and peas, alongside the house and attach the trellis to the house rather than depend on a freestanding support.

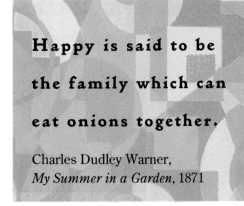

Happy is said to be the family which can eat onions together.

Charles Dudley Warner,
My Summer in a Garden, 1871

Place your containers where they will get plenty of sun, but keep in mind that soil in pots dries out faster than soil in the garden. And remember that plastic containers retain water better than clay or wood. Use a soil mix that drains well but is moisture retentive. Nona Koivula swears by a combination of peat, perlite and vermiculite, which she buys separately and mixes in her wheelbarrow. But she always throws in a handful of real soil. "I think it dries out less quickly if you have some soil in there," she says. I use Fafard potting soil laced with compost. Many experts recommend artificial soil mixes; most brands seem to work, and all should be replaced each year. What is unlikely to work well is a tub filled with garden soil.

With regular watering and a bimonthly shot of a water-soluble organic fertilizer (or a slow-release organic fertilizer worked into the soil

BASIC SOIL MIX FOR CONTAINERS

I PART . . . . .STERILE SOIL

I PART . . . . .COMPOST

I PART . . . . .PERLITE OR VERMICULITE

at planting time), your salad garden should be off and running. Container vegetables also respond to monthly foliar feedings of diluted manure or compost tea or fish emulsion. Weeding, thank heaven, is nearly optional.

CANDIDATES FOR THE CONTAINER GARDEN

Although almost any vegetable variety can be cultivated in a container, the varieties listed below are especially suited for tubs and pots because of their small size or compact growth habit.

BASIL:

'BALL BASIC'	'DWARF ITALIAN'	'GREEK MINIATURE'
'GREEN BUSH'	'SPICY GLOBE'	

BOK-CHOY:

'CHING CHIANG'	'MEI QING CHOY'

BROCCOLI:

'ATLANTIC'	'DANDY EARLY'	'GREEN COMET'

CABBAGE:

'EARLIANA'	'FAST BALL'	'HARBINGER'
'MINICOLE'		

CARROT:

'AMSTEL'	'BABY SPIKE'	'GOLDEN BALL'
'LITTLE FINGER'	'MINICOR'	'MOKUM'
'ORBIT'	'PARMEX'	'PLANET'
'THUMBELINA'		

CRESS:

'CRESSON'	'MOSS CURLED'	'UPLAND'

CAULIFLOWER:

'GARANT'	'PREDOMINANT'	'SNOWBABY'

CUCUMBER:

'BUSH CHAMPION'	'BUSH CROP'	'FANFARE'
'MINCU'	'POT LUCK'	'SALAD BUSH'
'SPACEMASTER'		

DILL:

'FERNLEAF'

ENDIVE:

'FINE MARAICHERE'	'GALIA'	'MOSS CURLED'

KALE:

'DWARF GREEN CURLED'	'SHOWBOR'

LETTUCE:

'BABY OAK'	'BIONDO LISCE'	'DAPPLE'
'GREEN ICE'	'GREEN MIGNONETTE'	'LITTLE GEM'
'LOLLO BIONDO'	'LOLLO ROSSA'	'MORGANA'
'RED LEPRECHAUN'	'ROUGETTE DU MIDI'	'SALINA'
'TOM THUMB'	'VALERIA'	'VASCO'

PARSLEY:

'CURLINA'	'EXTRA CURLED'
'EXTRA CURLED DWARF'	

PEA:

'EARLY PATIO'

PEPPER:

'GYPSY'

RADICCHIO:

'RED VERONA'	'SCILLA'

RADISH:

'CHERRY BELLE'	'COMET'	'EASTER EGG'
'FLUO'	'SPARKLER'	

SCALLION/GREEN ONION:

'RED BUNCHING'	'TOKYO BUNCHING'

SWEET PEPPER:

'ALBINO'	'JINGLE BELLS'

SWISS CHARD:

'COMPACTA SLOW BOLTING'

TOMATO:

'BETTER BUSH IMPROVED'	'GEM STATE'	'HUSKY GOLD'
'NORTHERN EXPOSURE'	'RED ROBIN'	'SMALL FRY'
'SUPER BUSH'	'TUMBLER'	'WHIPPERSNAPPER'
'YELLOW CANARY'		

TURNIP:

'MARKET EXPRESS'

ZUCCHINI SQUASH:

'BURPEE HYBRID'	'GOLDEN ROCKY'

THE INDOOR SALAD
Gardening in Jars

BY KATHLEEN FISHER

I N THE GLOOM OF WINTER, when the only available salad fixings seem to be cello-wrapped iceberg lettuce and genetically altered tomatoes, there's still one fresh, healthy and inexpensive ingredient you can grow yourself in two or three days in about a square foot of space on your kitchen counter: sprouts. (Of course you don't have to wait for winter; especially if you're a land-poor gardener, sprouts can help satisfy your vegetable-growing urge in any season.)

Sprouts don't earn rave reviews in every respect, however. They aren't nutritional powerhouses. While a respectable source of vitamins B and C and iron, sprouts have less protein by weight than most of the beans, grains and assorted seeds they spring from because so much of their bulk is water. Still, they score better than lettuce (0.9 grams protein per 100 gram for iceberg versus 3.1 grams for mung beans), and many sprouts, such as alfalfa and radish, weigh in at about a dozen calories per cup, which makes them far more guilt-free than popcorn.

Mung beans and alfalfa are the standard sprout fare in most supermarket produce sections, but the pos-

Sweet Vinaigrette

1/2 cup safflower oil
1/4 cup cider vinegar
2 Tbsp. honey
2 Tbsp. chopped chives
1 Tbsp. fresh lemon juice
1/2 tsp. sugar
Salt and freshly ground pepper

Combine all ingredients in a small bowl. Whisk until well blended. Salt and pepper to taste.

Alfalfa sprouts, along with many other kinds of sprouts, are a fresh, healthy and inexpensive salad ingredient that you can grow yourself in two or three days in about a square foot of space on your kitchen counter.

From left to right: mung beans, garbanzo beans and lentils. The list of seeds and beans that can be sprouted for salads goes on and on.

sibilities are much greater. Avoid any seeds intended for planting, though, since they are likely to have been treated with chemicals; instead, use beans and seeds sold for eating, found in grocery or health food stores. Oddly, the meat-and-potatoes males in my household prefer delicate little sprouts like alfalfa and clover. I like radish sprouts because of their peppery zip, reminiscent of a generous dab of horseradish. We all voted "yes" for the heirloom 'Calico Crowder' southern pea that I collected from a friend's garden. And the list goes on: clover, mustard, cress, turnip, fenugreek, cabbage, sunflower, onion, kale, kidney and navy bean, rye, wheat, soybean, lentil and more. The idea of buckwheat sprouts appealed to me—probably the result

> **Cabbages are extremely windy, whether you take them as Meat or as Medicine; yea, as windy Meat as can be eaten, unless you eat Bagpipes or Bellows....**
>
> Nicholas Culpeper,
> *The Compleat Herbal*, 1653

of childhood afternoons in front of the television watching "Little Rascals" reruns—but I had poor luck sprouting them. On the other hand, I was suspicious when a health food store manager told me that garbanzos sprout well, but indeed they do. You also can buy sprouting mixes; like all compromises, they please everyone a little. Or create your own mixes, keeping in mind that you want to mingle seeds that mature about the same time, such as alfalfa and peas or mustard and cabbage.

With all these decisions about *what* to sprout, it's reassuring to learn that you don't need any special equipment *to* sprout. If you're into gizmos, you can buy a special sprouter. I was given one that has four separate sprouting sections, and while it works well, it takes up too much space on my counter. Others swear by bamboo baskets and colanders covered with plastic-bag tents. Also recommended is a cloth sprouting bag (the best models are made of linen), which provides good drainage and aeration and is easy to use: Just immerse the seeds in water and hang it up. If you become hooked on sprouting, one of these devices is a good investment. But if a crop or two of cress per month is your limit, use the classic gear: a wide-mouth clear-glass jar set on its side with cheesecloth fas-

Buckwheat sprouts

tened over the top and secured with a rubberband. If you don't want to fuss with cheesecloth, there are screen lids available, or simply leave the top open. Jar, bag, basket or whatever, sprouting is nearly no-fail if you follow these steps:

- Soak seeds overnight
- Rinse and drain seeds; remove any chaff
- Wash jar and rinse with boiling water

- Spread seeds evenly in a single layer (don't overcrowd the container: 1 tablespoon of mung beans yields enough sprouts to fill a quart jar)
- Place jar in a cool spot where there is good air circulation and indirect light (sprouts such as cress that develop shoots and leaves, rather than just a root, need slightly more light in order to turn green)
- Rinse and drain seeds twice daily, keeping them damp but not wet

When you can see more sprouts than seeds, your crop is ready for harvest. Another sign is hull drop. With some sprouts, such as black sunflower, you'll

SEEDS FOR SPROUTING

SEED	LATIN NAME	EDIBLE PORTION
ADZUKI/ADUKI	*Vigna angularis*	BEAN & ROOT
ALFALFA	*Medicago sativa*	LEAF
CABBAGE	*Brassica oleracea,* Capitata group	LEAF
CHIVES	*Allium schoenoprasum, A. tuberosum*	SHOOT & ROOT
CLOVER	*Trifolium pratense, T. incarnatum*	LEAF
FENUGREEK	*Trigonella foenum-graecum*	LEAF
GARBANZO	*Cicer arietinum*	BEAN & ROOT
LENTIL	*Lens culinaris*	BEAN & ROOT
MUNG	*Vigna radiata*	BEAN & ROOT
MUSTARD	*Brassica nigra*	LEAF
PEAS	*Pisum sativum*	BEAN & ROOT
RADISH	*Raphanus sativus*	LEAF
BLACK SUNFLOWER	*Helianthus annuus*	LEAF

Sunflower sprouts

want to remove all the hulls before eating. Not only unpalatable, they tend to develop mold (get a head start by removing hulls each time you rinse the sprouts—the hulls tend to float). But play it by ear—the hulls of many sprouts, such as radish or onion, are so inconsequential that it's a waste of time to pick them out.

The rule of thumb for sprouts is storage time equals sprouting time. Sprouts with all hulls removed last longer than those that haven't been cleaned, but even in an airtight container, sprouts only keep about a week in the refrigerator. Seeds for sprouting should also be kept in an airtight container and stored in a cool, dark place for up to three months, or in the refrigerator or freezer for up to eight months.

One caveat: Any unpleasant odor or sign of mold and you should toss the crop. Unlike dirt farming, you can replant immediately, be harvesting in three days and never have to venture beyond your kitchen. All gardening should be so easy.

MATURE	FLAVOR	COMMENTS
3-5 DAYS	MILD	COUSIN OF MUNG
5-7 DAYS	MILD	WILL ROT IF IT GETS TOO HOT
3-5 DAYS	COLELIKE	REMOVE HULLS
10-14 DAYS	ONIONLIKE	SLOW TO SPROUT
4-6 DAYS	SLIGHT NIP	PRETTY LEAF, FAST TO MATURE
6-8 DAYS	BITTER	TALL, LIKES COOL TEMPERATURES
2-4 DAYS	HARDY	STEAM IF EATING IN QUANTITY
3-5 DAYS	HARDY	STEAM IF EATING IN QUANTITY
3-5 DAYS	MILD	DON'T BOTHER TO REMOVE HULLS
3-5 DAYS	PEPPERY	USE BLACK, NOT YELLOW MUSTARD
5-7 DAYS	MILD	AVOID SEED THAT HAS BEEN TREATED
3-5 DAYS	PEPPERY	EASY
6-10 DAYS	MILD	TALL; KEEP COOL; NEEDS EXTRA WATER

ADDING ZIP

Herbs
for the Salad

BY JANE GOOD

THE FOLKS IN EDEN might have been tempted to eat an apple, but I would have fallen for an herb. As old as time, ornamental and useful, perfumed and pungent, sweet and savory, most herbs are pest and disease free, and many are indispensable in salads.

You don't have to own a country estate to grow salad herbs. A garden the size of a kitchen table, even a large basket or barrel, can accommodate a reasonable selection. You can sow seeds of your favorites, either indoors for transplanting later or directly into the garden, but to make sure you get the best French tarragon, rosemary and Greek oregano, start with established plants from a reliable grower.

Herbs have only a few requirements: at least five hours of sun, protection from the wind (and frost, if they are tender plants), regular watering (but not so much that the ground is soggy) and well-drained, weed-free soil. Go easy on fertilizers: Too much nitrogen in the soil will reduce the volatile oils essential for good flavor and fragrance. Excessive washing of the foliage before use has the same effect. To maximize their oils, harvest herbs after the dew has dried, not before. And to keep the harvest coming, remove all flower buds before they open—the tender, new shoots that appear before plants bloom are generally most flavorful—and prune plants regularly to encourage lush growth.

> **[Parsley] is also an enemy of scorpions, and may be used as a potion to be spread on rabid dog-bites.**
>
> Leonardo da Vinci,
> *Leonardo's Kitchen Note Books*

Ornamental and useful, perfumed and pungent, sweet and savory, most herbs are pest and disease free, and many are indispensable in salads.

Above: Chives provide tender snips for salads from spring through fall. After the first flowering with edible pink blossoms, cut plants back to stimulate regrowth.

Left: Garlic is a long-season crop, so northern gardeners should plant it in the fall for harvest the following August. In warm climates, wait until spring to plant.

THE STARTING FIVE

Chives

My herb garden began with a gift pot of chives. The small clump of perennial, mildly onion-flavored, grassy leaves of *Allium schoenoprasum* grew well despite my horticultural naivete. Years later, handfuls of bulblets that spread from the original mound continue to thrive, and I've added other varieties, including garlic and mauve garlic chives. Now sequential harvests from many plants provide tender snips for salads from spring through fall. After the first flowering in June, when edible pink blossoms top the tough, hollow stalks, I cut the plants back to stimulate regrowth, saving the flowers to steep in bottles of sun-warmed white-wine vinegar. Garlic, or Chinese, chives (*A. tuberosum*) are a mildly garlic-flavored, equally useful and undemanding larger relative that bears white flowers in late summer.

Everyday Vinaigrette

1/2 cup olive oil
2 Tbsp. fresh lemon juice
1 Tbsp. balsamic vinegar
1 tsp. Dijon-style mustard
1 clove garlic, pressed

Combine all ingredients in a small jar. Cover and shake until well blended.

Garlic

Adherence to the culinary proverb, "Anything not benefitting from the addition of chocolate will probably benefit from the addition of garlic," is reason enough for me to grow ordinary *Allium sativum*. Moreover, garlic stores well and is space-efficient and inexpensive. Mail a few dollars to a garlic specialist and buy the beginnings of a lifetime supply of a reliable "reeking rose" or, after a taste test, barter with a garlic-growing neighbor to get a locally-adapted strain. Some chefs prefer the less pungent, top-setting rocambole, which is also known as Italian or serpent garlic (*A. sativum ophioscorodon*). The huge elephant garlic (*A. scorodoprasum*) is also mild but slightly more tricky to grow.

Garlic is a long-season crop, so northern gardeners should plant it in the fall for harvest the following August; those in warm climates can wait until spring. About the time of the first killing frost, push large cloves a few inches deep and 6 inches apart into a sunny bed of well-drained, rich, weed-free soil. Top-dress with compost and apply a foot of mulch. In the spring, pull the mulch away until the pale shoots are well-established, then reposition it to retain moisture and reduce weeds.

Garlic can be harvested in summer, but the keeping quality and flavor improve with maturity. I dig the bulbs once the tops have drooped and are beginning to turn brown, then dry them well and store in braids or net bags in a cool, dry, dark, well-ventilated place.

Dill

The ancients believed that "dill stayeth the hickets [hiccups]." True or not, this graceful, reliable annual stayeth in my garden. Generations of random self-seeders are as welcome as the newer compact cultivars, such as 'Bouquet' and 'Fernleaf', which I sow in rows. Common dill (*Anethum graveolens*) is a 3- to 5-foot relative of parsley that likes full sun, wind protection and light, well-drained soil. ('Sari' is an improved form, somewhat more aromatic.) Dill maintenance is minimal: Water, weed and thin to 8 inches. Because of its taproot, dill resists

Dill likes full sun, wind protection and light, well-drained soil.

Go easy on the fertilizers: Too much nitrogen in the soil reduces the volatile oils that give herbs their flavor and fragrance.

transplanting, so I eat the thinnings. Freshly cut dill is delicious. Both scissor-snipped baby dill (6-to-8-inch seedlings) and dill weed (older feathery foliage) taste mildly of licorice. Flowering reduces foliage growth, so remove the yellow heads and use them to garnish salads.

MORE HERBS FOR SALADS

Angelica, *Angelica archangelica*

Lemon balm, *Melissa officinalis*

Borage, *Borago officinalis*

Salad burnet, *Sanguisorba officinalis*

Chervil, *Anthriscus cereifolium*

Hyssop, *Hyssopus officinalis*

Lovage, *Levisticum officinale*

Marjoram, *Origanum* spp.

Mint, *Mentha* spp.

Sage, *Salvia officinalis*

Savory, *Satureja hortensis*

Sweet Cicely, *Myrrhis odorata*

Tarragon, *Artemisia dracunculus*

Thyme, *Thymus* spp.

Basil

Basil is the essence of summer, a necessary complement to an otherwise perfect tomato. Its clove-like flavor and fragrance, long associated with love, worship and madness, tempt gardeners to plant it everywhere. Witness decorative 'Lemon Gem', 'Green Ruffles' and 'Purple Ruffles' in the flower border; a 10-foot row of pungent 'Genovese' in the vegetable garden for an annual supply of pesto; and in a sidewalk planter, compact 'Spicy Globe', a small-leaved cultivar that admirably transplants summer to a winter windowsill. Despite the varietal possibilities—more than 40 varieties are widely available—the intensely-flavored common sweet basil (*Ocimum basilicum*), emerald-green and 18 inches tall, is still my choice for the salad bowl.

Basil is both easy to grow from seed and to transplant; however, it is a heat-loving tender annual, so protect it from frost. If you start with seed, watch out for "damping off," a fungus that topples seedlings like trees in a hurricane. I always start two dozen plants indoors in flats. About the time I transplant the seedlings—after the danger of frost—I also sow a second crop directly in the garden in warm, fertile, barely moist soil in an area with good air circulation. To harvest basil, cut entire branches before the flowers open and use the leaves. To maximize my harvest, I leave the suckers growing in the leaf axils—they give rise to new shoots—and fertilize monthly with manure tea or fish emulsion.

Parsley

Always plant parsley. Fresh parsley neutralizes the pungency of onions and garlic, enhances the flavors of other fresh herbs, gives dried herbs an almost-fresh taste and is rich in vitamins A and C. The ubiquitous curled, or French, parsley is more popular, but I prefer the rich-green color and robust flavor of Italian, or flat-leafed, parsley (*Petroselinum crispum* var. *neapolitanum*), which is also easier to cultivate and clean. I sow seed in late May directly into a relatively moist, partially shaded and sheltered corner of the vegetable garden where germination and growth are better (even without pre-soaking the seeds before planting) than in drier areas in full sun. Regular harvesting and occasional side-dressing with fish emulsion keep the plants productive. Parsley, which is a biennial, survives light frosts and, with adequate snow-cover, will reappear in spring, though many argue that its second-year flavor is harsh and strong. It can be potted for winter use indoors. ▣

From top: basil, Italian parsley and French parsley

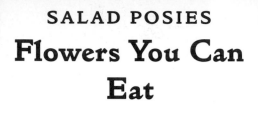

SALAD POSIES
Flowers You Can Eat

BY ROSALIND CREASY

I'D LOVE TO DESCRIBE the first flower I ate, but I can't remember it. Probably it was a nasturtium. I'm certain I started slowly—eating flowers wasn't mainline behavior 20 years ago. Then, at an herb seminar in 1983, I tasted anise hyssop blossoms in a salad. They were fantastic, and all my inhibitions disappeared.

Well, almost all my inhibitions. I'm still careful about what flowers I eat. Not all blossoms are edible, and dozens of bright flowers, all *looking* pretty enough to eat, are toxic. Foxglove, sweet pea, buttercup, morning glory, four o'clock, lily of the valley, daffodil and autumn crocus are but eight examples. Unless you're *absolutely* certain a flower is safe to eat, leave it out. People with serious allergies should approach flowers with caution, and no one should eat flowers that have been sprayed with chemicals, which includes flowers purchased from florist shops and nurseries.

That said, I've candied violets to use on cakes, made violet sorbet, steeped roses in honey to serve with baklava, deep fried batter-dipped squash blooms and sautéed daylilies. But those uses are limited. It was only when I began to use them in salads that flowers became part of my day-to-day cooking. Now I wouldn't serve a green salad that hasn't been brightened by a colorful flower or two. Sometimes I simply sprinkle a few nasturtiums over a lettuce salad; other times I feel inspired to make a flower confetti, mixing the petals, say, of calendulas, pansies and chives in a bowl and showering this kaleidoscope over a dressed bowl of greens.

> Celery, raw,
>
> Develops the jaw,
>
> But celery, stewed,
>
> Is more quietly
>
> chewed.
>
> Ogden Nash,
> "Celery," *Verses from 1929 On*,
> 1941.

As a general rule, I save flowers with strong flavors, such as anise hyssop and roses, to use as ingredients in dressings; flowers with small blooms, like borage and 'Lemon Gem' marigolds, I use whole, sprinkled over a salad or used as a garnish. With larger blossoms of plants like calendula and nasturtium, I separate the petals and add them to a flower confetti or leave the blooms intact and arrange

Edible flowers provide both color and flavor to a salad.

89

them around the salad bowl. In every case, they are spectacular.

Among the edible-flower adventures I'd just as soon forget are experiences that taught me the importance of cleaning blossoms well: An earwig emerging from a nasturtium is startling for both diner and cook. I've also learned that flower petals wilt readily, so make a petal confetti at the last minute and add it after the salad has been dressed.

The list of possibilities is long, but the following plants are my favorite edible flowers for salads. All are easily grown in most climates, and the choices include flowers for both cool and warm seasons. With the exception of squash, violas and pansies, which require a little pampering, these flowers need little fertilizer if grown in full sun and average garden soil.

Anise Hyssop (*Agastache foeniculum*)

A 3-foot, easily grown tender perennial with lavender flower spikes, anise hyssop has tiny but sweet anise-flavored petals that can be sprinkled over salads or incorporated into dressings. Start seeds indoors, five weeks before the last frost, or sow

Anise hyssop

directly in the garden after the danger of frost has passed. For a second crop of blossoms, cut back the spikes when the flowers have faded.

Borage (*Borago officinalis*)

Borage is one of the easiest annual summer herbs to grow; sow seeds outdoors after the last-frost date. Normally about 2 feet tall, it can grow twice that tall in mild-climate gardens like mine. The drooping flowers are deep-blue, half-inch stars with a slight cucumber taste. Remove the sepals (the hairy

Borage

outer flower parts that encase the flower bud) before using the flower. While they add little flavor, the blue blossoms are striking when sprinkled over salads.

Calendula (*Calendula officinalis*)

Calendulas, or pot marigolds, are one-foot cool-season annuals with one-inch orange and yellow flowers. Sow seed directly in the garden

Calendula

Rosemary

after all danger of frost has passed. Although they pack a slight tang, I use them primarily for color, not flavor. Remove petals from the heads before using them to brighten a salad.

Common and Garlic Chives
(Allium schoenoprasum, A. tuberosum)

Both common and garlic, or Chinese, chives are perennial second cousins of onions and can be grown easily from seed. The cloverlike flowers of common chives are lavender and appear in spring; garlic chives have larger white flat flower clusters in summer. I harvest the flowers just after they open, well before they become "papery," then pull the small florets off the flower heads and use when a mild chive or onion taste is called for.

Coriander

Culinary Herbs

All culinary herb flowers can be eaten, but many, such as burnet and oregano, are so tiny that they are not worth the trouble. The most versatile herb flowers are coriander (*Coriandrum sativum*), dill (*Anethum graveolens*), fennel (*Foeniculum vulgare*) and mint (*Mentha* spp.); here, small sections of the flower spray can be cut off and sprinkled over salads. Sage (*Salvia officinalis*), rosemary (*Rosmarinus officinalis*) and basil (*Ocimum* spp.) blossoms can be used in the same way. All herb blossoms taste like a mild form of the herb and are primarily useful in a flower confetti or as an edible garnish.

FLOWERS FOR EATING

Anise Hyssop, *Agastache foeniculum*
Basil, *Ocimum* spp.
Bee Balm, *Monarda didyma*
Borage, *Borago officinalis*
Calendula, *Calendula officinalis*
Chamomile, *Chamaemelum nobile*
Chicory, *Cichorium intybus*
Chrysanthemum, *Chrysanthemum* spp.
Common Chives, *Allium schoenoprasum*
Coriander, *Coriandrum sativum*
Daylily, *Hemerocallis* spp.
Dianthus, *Dianthus caryophyllus*
Dill, *Anethum graveolens*
English Daisy, *Bellis perennis*
Fennel, *Foeniculum vulgare*
Garlic Chives, *Allium tuberosum*
Honeysuckle, *Lonicera japonica*
Johnny-jump-up, *Viola tricolor*
Marigold, *Tagetes* spp.
Mint, *Mentha* spp.
Mustard, *Brassica* spp.
Nasturtium, *Tropaeolum minor*
Pansy, *Viola* x *wittrockiana*
Pea, *Pisum sativum*
Red Clover, *Trifolium pratense*
Rose, *Rosa* spp.
Rosemary, *Rosmarinus officinalis*
Runner Bean, *Phaseolus coccineus*
Sage, *Salvia officinalis*
Squash, *Cucurbita* spp.
Sweet Woodruff, *Galium odoratum*
Tulip, *Tulipa* spp.
Viola, *Viola cornuta*
Violet, *Viola odorata*

Nasturtiums

Yogurt Dressing

2/3 cup plain yogurt
1 Tbsp. Dijon-style mustard
1 Tbsp. fresh lemon juice
1 Tbsp. olive oil
1 Tbsp. chopped fresh
parsley or chives
Salt and freshly ground
pepper to taste

In a small bowl, combine mustard, lemon juice and yogurt. Add oil, stirring until well blended. Stir in parsely or chives and salt and pepper to taste. Chill 1 hour before serving.

Nasturtium (*Tropaeolum minor*)

Nasturtiums, which usually grow to about 10 inches tall but twice that wide, are annuals with yellow, red or orange flowers. Sow seeds outdoors on or a week before the frost-free date. The blooms, which have a peppery watercress flavor, are great sprinkled over salads. Be sure to wash each flower carefully: the tail-like spur is a favorite hiding place of aphids and other insects. Nasturtium leaves, reminiscent of cress, are also edible.

Clean edible blossoms well; an earwig emerging from a nasturtium is startling for both diner and cook.

Scarlet runner bean

Runner Bean (*Phaseolus coccineus*)

Runner bean flowers, colored coral or white, grow on tall annual vines. The blooms have a subtle bean flavor, and each contains a drop or two of sweet nectar. Plant this annual as you would any bean—after the danger of frost has passed—and be sure to give the vines some kind of support. I top salads with individual flowers or add the petals to a flower confetti. To keep the plants producing flowers, pick any beans that form.

Viola, Pansy and Johnny-jump-up (*Viola cornuta*, *V.* x *wittrockiana*, *V. tricolor*)

These three lovely small *Viola*, which grow easily from seed and often self-seed, are cool-weather annuals. They bloom in numerous hues—both single and bicolors—and taste rather like lettuce. The individual petals of the larger pansy are striking when used in a confetti sprinkled over green salads; Johnny-jump-ups and violas are better used whole.

Pansies

Seed Sources

ALFREY SEEDS
P.O. Box 415
Knoxville, TN 37901
Pepper specialists, especially chile
varieties. Seed list for SASE.

W. ATLEE BURPEE & CO.
300 Park Avenue
Warminster, PA 18974
Wide selection of vegetables and
flowers. Catalog free.

ALLEN, STERLING & LOTHROP
191 U.S. Rte. 1
Falmouth, ME 04105-1385
Standard varieties of vegetables and
flowers. Catalog $1, refundable with
order.

BUTTERBROOKE FARM
78 Barry Road
Oxford, CT 06483
Untreated, open-pollinated vegetable
seeds grown using bio-dynamic
methods. Seed list $1.

BERLIN SEEDS
5371 County Road 77
Millersbury, OH 44654
Standard varieties of vegetables and
flowers. Catalog free.

COMPANION PLANTS
7246 North Coolville Ridge Road
Athens, OH 45701
Culinary, medicinal and ornamental
herbs. Catalog $3.

BOUNTIFUL GARDENS SEEDS
18001 Shafer Ranch Road
Willits, CA 95490
Heirloom vegetable specialist;
untreated seeds. Catalog free.

THE COOK'S GARDEN
P.O. Box 535
Londonderry, VT 05148
Salad-garden specialist. Catalog free.

CROSS SEED CO.
109 9th St.
Bunker Hill, KS 67626
Seeds for sprouting. Price list $1,
refundable with order.

DEGIORGI SEED COMPANY
6011 N St.
Omaha, NE 68117-1634
Wide selection of vegetables and
flowers. Catalog $2.

DEEP DIVERSITY
P.O. Box 15189
Santa Fe, NM 87506-5189
Open-pollinated vegetables and
flowers. Catalog $4.

DOWN ON THE FARM SEED
P.O. Box 184
Hiram, OH 44234
Open-pollinated standard and
heirloom varieties. Catalog free.

EVERGREEN Y.H. ENTERPRISES
P.O. Box 17538
Anaheim, CA 92817
Asian vegetables. Catalog $2,
refundable with order.

FEDCO SEEDS
P.O. Box 520
Waterville, ME 04903
Untreated vegetable and flower seeds
for cold short seasons. Catalog $2.

FIELD & FOREST PRODUCTS, INC.
N3296 Kozuzerk Road
Peshitigo, WI 54157
Mushroom specialist. Catalog $2,
refundable with order.

FILAREE FARM
Rt. 2, Box 162
Okanogan, WA 98840
Garlic specialist. Catalog $2.

FUNGI PERFECTI
P.O. Box 7634
Olympia, WA 98507
Mushroom specialist. Catalog $3,
refundable with order.

GARDEN CITY SEEDS
1324 Red Crow Road
Victor, MT 59875
Cold-tolerant, untreated vegetables
and flowers. Catalog free.

THE GOURMET GARDENER
8650 College Boulevard
Overland Park, KS 66210
Vegetables and edible flowers from
around the world. Catalog $2,
refundable with order.

HARRIS SEEDS
60 Saginaw Drive
Rochester, NY 14623
Wide selection of vegetables and
flowers. Catalog free.

HIGH ALTITUDE GARDENS-SEEDS TRUST
P.O. Box 1048
Hailey, ID 83333
Vegetables and flowers for short, cool
seasons.
Catalog $3, refundable with order.

J.L. HUDSON, SEEDSMAN
P.O. Box 1058
Redwood City, CA 94064
Uncommon vegetables and flowers
from around the world. Catalog $1.

JOHNNY'S SELECTED SEEDS
Foss Hill Road
Albion, ME 04910
Wide selection of vegetables and
flowers. Catalog free.

J.W. JUNG SEED CO.
Randloph, WI 53957
Wide selection of vegetables and
flowers. Catalog free.

KITAZAWA SEED COMPANY
1111 Chapman St.
San Jose, CA 95126
Asian vegetables. Catalog free.

KALMIA FARM
P.O. Box 3881
Charlottesville, VA 22903-0881
Shallots, hardy multiplier and
topsetting onions. Catalog free.

LE JARDIN DU GOURMET
P.O. Box 7H
St. Johnsbury Center, VT 05863
European vegetable varieties
specialist. Catalog free.

LIBERTY SEED COMPANY
Box 805
New Philadelphia, OH 44663
Wide selection of vegetables and
herbs. Catalog free.

MEADOWBROOK HERB GARDEN
93 Kingstown Road
Wyoming, RI 02898
Herb specialist. Price list for SASE.

NATIVE SEEDS/SEARCH
2059 No. Campbell #325
Tucson, AZ 85719
Traditional Southwestern vegetables.
Catalog $1.

NICHOLS GARDEN NURSERY
1190 No. Pacific Hwy.
Alband, OR 97321-4580
Vegetables and herbs for the Pacific
Northwest. Catalog free.

PARK SEED CO.
Cokesbury Road
Greenwood, SC 29647-0001
Wide selection of vegetables and
flowers. Catalog free.

PINETREE GARDEN SEEDS
P.O. Box 300
New Gloucester, ME 04260
Wide selection of vegetables and
flowers. Catalog free.

SEEDS BLÜM
Idaho City Stage
Boise, ID 83706
Open-pollinated and heirloom
vegetable specialist. Catalog $3.

PLANTS OF THE SOUTHWEST
Agua Fria, Rt. 6, Box 11-A
Santa Fe, NM 87501
Traditional Southwestern vegetables
and flowers. Catalog $3.50.

SEEDS OF CHANGE
621 Old Santa Fe Trail #10
Santa Fe, NM 87501
Open-pollinated heirloom and native
vegetables, herbs and flowers. Catalog
free.

REDWOOD CITY SEED COMPANY
P.O. Box 361
Redwood City, CA 94064
Endangered and traditional
vegetables. Catalog $1.

SEEDS WEST GARDEN SEEDS
P.O. Box 27057
Albuquerque, NM 87125-7075
Short-season vegetables, flowers and
herbs. Catalog free.

RICHTERS
357 Hwy. 47, Goodwood,
ONT L0C 1A0
Canada
Herb specialist. Catalog $2.

SHEPHERD'S GARDEN SEEDS
6116 Highway 9
Felton, CA 95018-9709
Gourmet vegetables and flowers.
Catalog free.

SEED SAVERS EXCHANGE
Flower and Herb Exchange
3076 North Winn Road
Decorah, IA 52101
Cooperative; open-pollinated
vegetables, flowers and herbs.
Information on SSE $1;
information on FHE free.

SOUTHERN EXPOSURE SEED EXCHANGE
P.O. Box 170
Earlysville, VA 22936
Heirloom vegetables and flowers for
southern gardens. Catalog $2,
refundable with order.

SOUTHERN SEEDS
P.O. Box 2091
Melbourne, FL 32902
Open-pollinated vegetables for
southern gardens. Catalog $1.

STOKES SEEDS INC.
Box 548
Buffalo, NY 14240-0548
Wide selection of vegetables and
flowers. Catalog free.

TERRITORIAL SEED COMPANY
P.O. Box 157
Cottage Grove, OR 97424
Vegetables for year-round gardening.
Catalog free.

THOMPSON AND MORGAN
Dept PR95
Jackson, NJ 08527
Wide selection of flowers and
vegetables. Catalog free.

**TOMATO GROWERS SUPPLY
COMPANY**
P.O. Box 2237
Fort Myers, FL 33902
Catalog free.

THE TOMATO SEED COMPANY, INC.
P.O. Box 1400
Tryon, NC 28782
Catalog free.

TOTALLY TOMATOES
P.O. Box 1626
Augusta, GA 30903
Catalog free.

TWILLEY SEED COMPANY
P.O. Box 65
Trevose, PA 19053
Wide selection of hybrid vegetables.
Catalog free.

VESEY'S SEEDS LTD.
York, PEI C0A 1P0
Canada
Vegetables and flowers for short
seasons. Catalog free.

FURTHER READING

Barash, Cathy Wilkinson. *Edible Flowers: From Garden to Palate* (Fulcrum Publishing, 1993)

Coleman, Eliot. *The New Organic Grower's Four-Season Harvest* (Chelsea Green, 1992)

Evelyn, John. *Acetaria: A Discourse of Sallets* (University of Virginia Press, 1983)

Forsyth, Turid, and Merilyn Simonds Mohr. *The Harrowsmith Salad Garden* (Camden House Publishing, 1992)

Meyerowitz, Steve. *Sprout It!* (The Sprout House, Inc., 1994)

Nathan, Amy. *Salad* (Chronicle Books, 1985)

Proulx, E. Annie. *The Fine Art of Salad Gardening* (Rodale Press, 1985)

Cachepot: The Container Vegetable Gardener's Companion (For a subscription, write: Cornucopia Press, 3 Golf Center, Suite 221, Hoffman Estates, IL 60195; $15/year)

CONTRIBUTORS

ROSALIND CREASY, one of the early champions of edible landscaping, is the author of *Cooking from the Garden* (Sierra Club Books, 1988).

KARAN DAVIS CUTLER, guest editor for this handbook, is the managing editor of *Harrowsmith Country Life* magazine. She wages a never-ending battle with Vermont's stoney soil.

PAUL DUNPHY is a contributing editor at *Harrowsmith Country Life* magazine. He lives and gardens in western Massachusetts.

SYDNEY EDDISON, the author of *A Patchwork Garden* (Henry Holt, 1992), has just completed a book about gardeners in winter, *The Unsung Season* (Houghton Mifflin, 1995).

KATHLEEN FISHER gardens in Virginia and is the editor of *American Horticulturist*, a publication of the American Horticultural Society.

JANE GOOD, the editor of *The Gardener's Color Guide* (Camden House, 1993), cultivates herbs and other edibles between limestone ridges in eastern Ontario, a setting that challenges the grower and her plants.

CASS PETERSON, a former environmental writer for the *Washington Post*, is a market gardener in Pennsylvania, where she grows more than 60 varieties of tomatoes.

DEBORAH WECHSLER lives in the North Carolina Piedmont, where she is an occasional market gardener and regular freelance writer.

PHOTO CREDITS

Cover and pages 1, 4, 7, 8, 15, 17, 19, 20, 23 top and bottom, 28, 30, 32 top, 37, 40, 42, 45, 49, 66, 80, 85, 88, 96 bottom, 101 by **ROSALIND CREASY**

Pages 6, 13, 59, 62, 63, 72, 76 left, middle and right, 78, 79, 98 by **CHRISTINE M. DOUGLAS**

Pages 10, 32 bottom, 34 top and bottom, 38 top and bottom, 54, 64, 82 top and bottom, 84, 87 top and middle, 90, 91 top and bottom, 92 top and bottom, 94, 95, 96 top by **CATHY WILKINSON BARASH**

Pages 14, 22 top and bottom, 44 middle and bottom, 53, 55, 56, 57, 58, 61, 68, 70 by **JUDYWHITE**

Page 44 top by **ALAN L. DETRICK**

Page 87 bottom by **KARAN DAVIS CUTLER**

INDEX

Gardening Books for the Next Century from the Brooklyn Botanic Garden

Don't miss any of the gardening books in Brooklyn Botanic Garden's 21st-Century Gardening Series! Published four times a year, these acclaimed books explore the frontiers of ecological gardening—offering practical, step-by-step tips on creating environmentally sensitive and beautiful gardens for the 1990s and the new century. Your subscription to BBG's 21st-Century Gardening Series is free with Brooklyn Botanic Garden membership.

FOR INFORMATION ON ORDERING ANY OF THE FOLLOWING BACK TITLES, PLEASE WRITE THE BROOKLYN BOTANIC GARDEN AT THE ABOVE ADDRESS OR CALL (718) 622-4433, EXT. 274.

American Cottage Gardening
Annuals: A Gardener's Guide
Bonsai: Special Techniques
Butterfly Gardens
Culinary Herbs
Easy-care Roses
The Environmental Gardener
Ferns
Garden Photography
The Gardener's World of Bulbs
Gardening for Fragrance
Gardening in the Shade

Gardening with Wildflowers
  & Native Plants
Going Native: Biodiversity
  in Our Own Backyards
Greenhouses & Garden Rooms
Herbs & Cooking
Herbs & Their Ornamental Uses
Hollies: A Gardener's Guide
Indoor Bonsai
Japanese Gardens
The Natural Lawn & Alternatives
Natural Insect Control
A New Look at Vegetables

A New Look at Houseplants
Orchids for the Home
  & Greenhouse
Ornamental Grasses
Perennials: A Gardener's Guide
Pruning Techniques
Roses
Shrubs: The New Glamour Plants
Soils
The Town & City Gardener
Trees: A Gardener's Guide
Water Gardening
The Winter Garden